D1459972

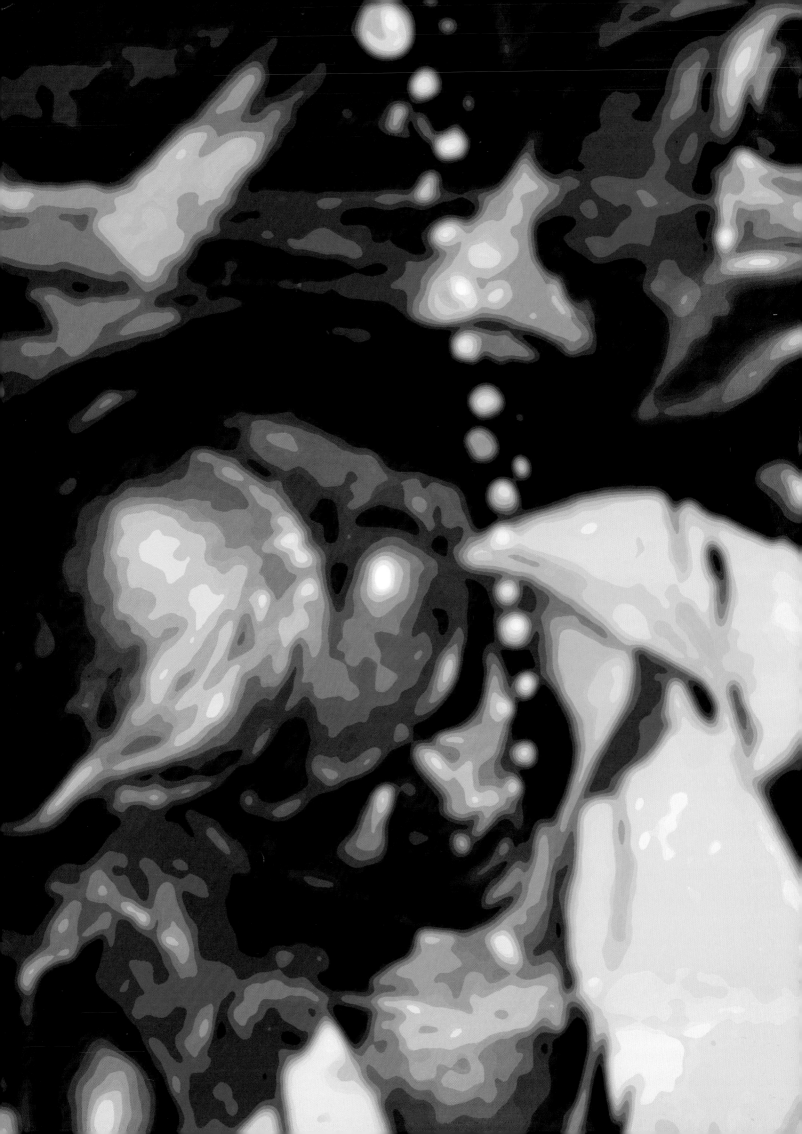

MASTER STORYTELLER

by
William J. Widder

Preface by
Frank Kelly Freas

AN ILLUSTRATED TOUR OF THE FICTION OF

L. RON HUBBARD

GALAXY
PRESS

Galaxy Press, LLC
7051 Hollywood Boulevard, Suite 200
Hollywood, California 90028

telephone: (323) 466-7815
facsimile: (323) 466-7817
www.galaxypress.com

ISBN 1-59212-054-7

New Era Publications International ApS
Store Kongensgade 53
1264 Copenhagen K, Denmark

telephone: (45) 33 73 66 66
facsimile: (45) 33 73 66 33
www.newerapublications.com

ISBN 87-7989-522-0

Design: AutHaus

Printed in the United States of America
2 3 4 5 6 7 8 9 10

Library of Congress Control Number: 2003103675

ACKNOWLEDGMENTS

I would like, first, to acknowledge the following institutions, organizations and resources for their assistance in making available valuable background, reference and corollary materials about the life and work of L. Ron Hubbard in the writing of this book:

University Research Library, University of California at Los Angeles; the Doheny Memorial Library, University of Southern California, Los Angeles; Huntington Library, San Marino, California; University of California at Riverside, Riverside, California; and the Charles Von der Ahe Library, Loyola Marymount University, Los Angeles. I would also like to thank the Beinecke Rare Book and Manuscript Library, Yale University, New Haven, Connecticut; the Butler Library, Columbia University, New York City; the Widener Library, Harvard University, Cambridge, Massachusetts; the Center for the Study of Science Fiction, University of Kansas, Lawrence, Kansas; the Library of Congress; the Smithsonian Institute Libraries; and The George Washington University, Washington, D.C.

A special debt of gratitude is owed, as well, to the L. Ron Hubbard Library, the L. Ron Hubbard Life Exhibition and Author Services, all of Hollywood, California, for their generous and indispensable assistance.

And, finally, I would like to thank my wife, Beverly, and my son, Frank, for their unfailingly enthusiastic help and support.

William Widder
Los Angeles
May 2003

TABLE OF CONTENTS

PREFACE —— ii

INTRODUCTION ———————————————————————————————————— iv

PULP FICTION

HIGH ROAD TO ADVENTURE ——————————————————————————— 1

DANGER IS MY BUSINESS ———————————————————————————— 9

THE "HELL JOB" SERIES ———————————————————————————— 26

CRIME DOESN'T PAY ————————————————————————————————— 35

THE OLD WEST COMES ALIVE ——————————————————————— 41

THE GOLDEN AGE OF SCIENCE FICTION

CHANGING A GENRE ——————————————————————————————————— 51

INTO THE UNKNOWN—AND BEYOND ——————————————————— 68

"HATS AND BATS AND CATS" ————————————————————————— 78

OTHER WORLDS ——————————————————————————————————————— 90

THE CONQUEST OF SPACE ———————————————————————————— 104

BATTLEFIELD EARTH ——————————————————————————————— 113

MISSION EARTH ——————————————————————————————————————— 129

WORLDS OF TOMORROW ——————————————————————————————— 145

L. RON HUBBARD

A BIOGRAPHICAL CHRONOLOGY ——————————————————————— 163

THE FICTION OF L. RON HUBBARD ———————————————— 183

POSTSCRIPT ——— 191

INDEX —— 192

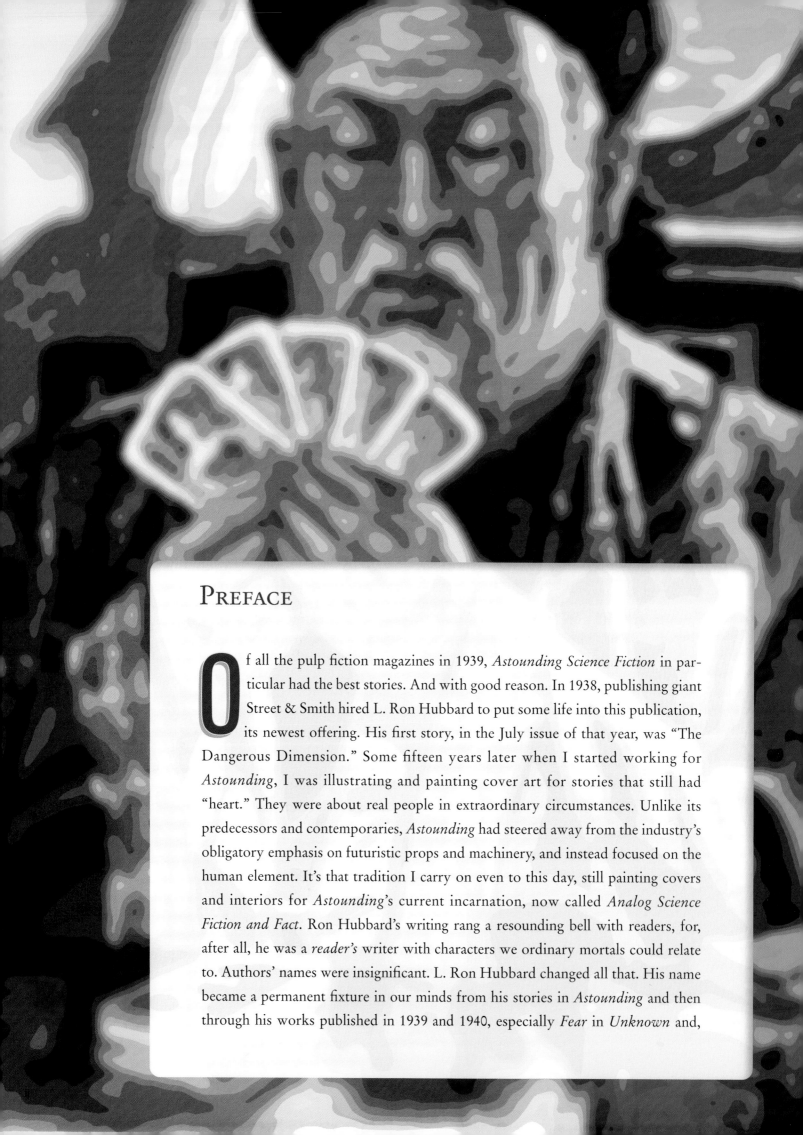

PREFACE

O f all the pulp fiction magazines in 1939, *Astounding Science Fiction* in particular had the best stories. And with good reason. In 1938, publishing giant Street & Smith hired L. Ron Hubbard to put some life into this publication, its newest offering. His first story, in the July issue of that year, was "The Dangerous Dimension." Some fifteen years later when I started working for *Astounding*, I was illustrating and painting cover art for stories that still had "heart." They were about real people in extraordinary circumstances. Unlike its predecessors and contemporaries, *Astounding* had steered away from the industry's obligatory emphasis on futuristic props and machinery, and instead focused on the human element. It's that tradition I carry on even to this day, still painting covers and interiors for *Astounding*'s current incarnation, now called *Analog Science Fiction and Fact*. Ron Hubbard's writing rang a resounding bell with readers, for, after all, he was a *reader's* writer with characters we ordinary mortals could relate to. Authors' names were insignificant. L. Ron Hubbard changed all that. His name became a permanent fixture in our minds from his stories in *Astounding* and then through his works published in 1939 and 1940, especially *Fear* in *Unknown* and, above all, *Final Blackout*. He continued writing for *Astounding* until 1950, just before I began painting covers for that magazine.

In the early 1980s, after a thirty-year hiatus from fiction writing, Hubbard returned to science fiction and produced more blockbuster bestsellers—*Battlefield Earth* and the ten-volume *Mission Earth* series. He'd never lost his touch. I found myself, page after page after page, wanting to know what happened next. The sense of excitement, of really being there, of wanting to know more, was as strong then as in his early days. And, happily, these later works earned him numerous awards of distinction and recognition and elevated his already lofty legacy.

I wish I'd had the opportunity to become more closely acquainted with Ron. We met a few times in person, the first being in *Astounding* editor John W. Campbell's office. But I know this—he was a gentleman as well as a literary force, with the capacity to make an acquaintance feel important and a friend seem cherished.

I saw Ron in action a few times in Campbell's office. He seemed to be always ready to help any struggling young writer and once I actually clocked one of these discussions at thirty-seven minutes! No professional back then had that kind of time to spare—including, or maybe especially, Ron, but he took that time whenever it was needed. More than a writer, more than an adventurer, Ron was one of the finest of all, a truly human being.

It was his devotion to helping promising new writers and illustrators that inspired L. Ron Hubbard to establish the Writers and Illustrators of the Future Contests. He sensed what he defined as a "creative synergy" between the written word and the art that illustrates it. He knew that each standing alone, while superb in its own right, is the poorer for want of the other, for together they create a whole greater than the sum of its parts.

It was my privilege and pleasure to have served as the illustrator contest's Coordinating Judge for the first seven years after its inception in 1988. Both contests have launched the careers of some of today's most talented published authors and artists in science fiction and fantasy, thus providing a lasting contribution to the publishing world as well as a great gift for readers everywhere. Their annual published volumes, *L. Ron Hubbard Presents Writers of the Future*, even have a couple of my paintings on the covers. I'm glad the publisher used some of my better work for those covers. I feel I owe it to Ron.

When L. Ron Hubbard left this world in 1986, a great void was created in the fields of writing, art, film and music. His kind is likely never to be seen again.

With greatest respect and admiration,

Frank Kelly Freas

INTRODUCTION

This book, at its nostalgic heart, is the record of a personal journey that began for me on a day in April 1936. We were living in a New York City apartment, and with twenty-five cents that I had somehow cajoled from my mother (the Depression still lay athwart the land, and a quarter was no bagatelle) I walked the two or two and a half city blocks to the nearest corner newsstand.

The ubiquitous American newsstand of those days was an event. There were the mounds of newspapers, with the black-on-white quilting of headlines and pictures, of course. But far beyond that, for me assuredly, was the opulent caravan of pulp fiction magazines and their sensational cover art, inviting me, drawing me, irresistibly, to a world of adventure and action, mystery and suspense—distant, different, strange and wonderful. I cannot precisely remember, now, why—out of that kaleidoscope of color and boldly imperative story titles—my attention fixed on a magazine called *Mystery Novels*. But, felicitously, it did—and my grand adventure into the Age of Pulp Fiction began.

I have a sense that I flipped through the pages—there was a kind of initiatory ritual about it: the inimitable feel of the wood-pulp paper and its rugged edges, and the distinct redolence of the ink. But the story I stopped at, the one I then read compulsively as I walked home, was "The Death Flyer" by L. Ron Hubbard, who was already familiar to millions of readers of marquee magazines like *Top-Notch* and *Adventure* and *Five Novels Monthly*.

I read "The Death Flyer" again not too long ago, still appreciative of its lucid, sharp-edged, absorbingly straight-at-you Hubbard style. And more than sixty years after that walk home, my breath caught again, and held, as it had the first time, when the hero tried vainly (though I already knew it, yet wanted the outcome, somehow, to change) to alter the destinies of those aboard a passenger train—a "Death Flyer"—doomed to crash, irrevocably and forever in time. The impact of the story on me was immediate and pronounced and, as it has turned out, a deeply lasting one.

L. Ron Hubbard's "Death Flyer" opened a new, vivid, endlessly fascinating world of reading for me: a world that changed dramatically every month, that fired expectation and left me, invariably, hungry for more. I found my way to other writers, of course, sampling, as I went along, Hammett, Burroughs and Sabatini, I recall, and a smattering of "Doc Savage" and "The Shadow," a bit of Max Brand and some Lovecraft and Verne. But it was Hubbard I followed tenaciously to his British man-of-war seafaring classic "Mr. Tidwell, Gunner," and "Six-Gun Caballero" and "Arctic Wings"; to his watershed hardcover novel of the early Northwest frontier, *Buckskin Brigades*, and a full literary spectrum of other stories. I followed him also to magazines that were unmistakably among the aristocrats of the field, *Adventure* and *Western Story*, *Phantom Detective*, *Five Novels* and *Top-Notch*. And, of course, to pulp fiction's patriarch, *Argosy*, and L. Ron Hubbard's celebrated "Hell Job" series on the world's most uninsurably dangerous occupations—a first in the magazine's history. I read these with avidity at the time; they imaginatively extended the boundaries of the world I lived in and I have, with no small affection, explored them at length later in this volume.

Then, with his mastery of the storytelling art already in sharp focus across the breadth of popular fiction, Hubbard brought his versatile skills to a new field—and with enduring and far-reaching repercussions. His first science fiction story,

"The Dangerous Dimension," appeared in the July 1938 issue of the newly revamped magazine *Astounding Science Fiction*—and with it came a tectonic shift in the genre, a change in its shape and course, one that moved away from insensate machines and bristling vortex blasters to the most dangerous dimension of all—the mind. A new era had, indeed, begun and it would grow and flower, with Heinlein and van Vogt, Williamson and Asimov, into the fabled golden age and, beyond, into the quintessential fabric, the very matrix, of modern speculative fiction.

L. Ron Hubbard (circa 1930) at the outset of a career that would span more than half a century of trendsetting literary production.

The short story "**The Death Flyer**" appeared in this issue of *Mystery Novels Magazine*, April 1936. It is Ron's earliest known blending of hard-hitting adventure, mystery and the supernatural.

L. Ron Hubbard, as one distinguished author and literary historian recently put it, was, in fact, "the sort of intensive phenomenon who appears once in a lifetime, in effect makes his own rules, and transforms everything around him." No one then, he added, and no one subsequently "could discuss science fiction without discussing him." For me, and for a legion of others like me, no one did.

What came next after Hubbard's speculative fiction debut was a wide, brilliantly lighted concourse of landmark science fiction and fantasy. There was "The Tramp" and *Slaves of Sleep*, and then the monumental outpouring of *Fear*, *Final Blackout*, *Typewriter in the Sky*, *Death's Deputy* and *The Indigestible Triton*, all in 1940, framing an entire literary decade in a single year, indelibly marking a genre and reshaping its future. There were the later startlingly innovative works *The End Is Not Yet* and *Ole Doc Methuselah*, *The Masters of Sleep* and the time-and-space-vaulting *To the Stars*. And, finally, decades later, the jewels in the crown, the culminating trendsetters and record breakers, *Battlefield Earth* and the vast *Mission Earth* series—hugely imagined, action swept, memorably detailed in their characters, events and settings, threaded with finely tuned wit and piercing satire, and urging us with narrative skill to explore the themes that run vividly through the larger body of his work—valor, integrity, loyalty, compassion and the indestructibility of the human spirit.

There were, of course, many other L. Ron Hubbard novels and stories in this wide gallery of fiction, stories that created for millions of readers the sense of the real, and romantic, old West and the hard-edged tone of cities. The feel and perilous tempo of life at sea, or the sharp exhilaration of flight. Or the cloistering fear of what may lie waiting for us, in the corner, muted in shadow. Or the ineffable challenges of other worlds and other futures, and voyages through the limitless caverns of time and space.

I said at the outset that this book represents a momentous personal journey for me. But it is surely one for you, also. It is a journey teeming with excitement, illumined by a writer's surpassing craftsmanship and his telling insight into human nature, and stirring with the people, places and events of this day and moment, and of other times, and of worlds to come.

Join me.

PULP FICTION

HIGH ROAD TO ADVENTURE

When L. Ron Hubbard's first commercially published story, "The Green God," appeared in *Thrilling Adventures'* February 1934 edition, it marked not so much the debut of a new writer as it did the emergence of a literary force. And what would be clear in a matter of months—it was one with a capacity for rapid-fire production in extraordinary volume. In less than a year, in the words of one of publishing's most esteemed periodicals, Hubbard earned a reputation "as a superlative storyteller with total mastery of plot and pacing."

It was all there from the first—taut action, memorably defined characters, vivid plot contours, compelling artistry and that hallmark Hubbard sense of authenticity. His tales delivered a sharp jolt of reality drawn from a wealth of his own experience in a life that, at only twenty-three, was already the widely traveled, richly diverse, boldly adventurous stuff of which towering careers—and legends—are made.

Thrilling Adventures was an all-story "pulp" magazine, printed on rough, unfinished paper stock with untrimmed edges. Embellished by colorful, melodramatic cover art and evocative black-and-white interior illustrations, the pulps had a distinctive "feel" and redolence that was an indelible part of the reading experience. *Thrilling Adventures* was among the most popular of the hundreds of pulps that crowded the shelves of tens of thousands of newsstands nationwide, commanding more than thirty million readers—more than a quarter of the U.S. population—every month. Their panorama of literary genres—action and adventure, western and frontier, mystery and detective, air and sea yarns, Foreign Legion, U.S. Marines, explorers and gunslingers, prospectors and smugglers—both epitomized and defined one of the most extraordinary cultural and social phenomena of the twentieth century.

Like jazz and baseball, pulp fiction was a uniquely American invention, with its roots in the national experience tracing back to the 1830s, when four-page story weeklies printed on newsprint became the inexpensive reading fare of a westward

Ron in Washington, D.C., circa 1931. An author at the start of a fifty-year career.

"Wind-Gone-Mad," published in October 1935.

2

"Hurricane's Roar," published in April 1939.

"The Old Mill," as Hubbard affectionately dubbed his classic Remington.

migrating population. Cheaper paper available in larger quantities, faster presses, a more efficient postal service, transcontinental commerce and travel by railroad led to the appearance of the thirty-two-page dime novel and the introduction to the American psyche of a gallery of enduring literary heroes, both real and imagined, including Buffalo Bill, Frank Merriwell, Tom Swift, Horatio Alger and Nick Carter.

From that heritage, and for an increasingly literate twentieth-century American population, the pulp fiction magazine arose and flourished and changed the course and complexion of America's popular culture. The pulp was born in 1896 when publisher Frank Munsey changed the name of a failing children's magazine—*The Golden Argosy*—to *The Argosy* (and later, simply, to *Argosy*), and offered urgent yellow covers and more than a hundred pages of fiction—some 130,000 words— for a dime. The market for it was ready, waiting and enormous. Millions of people eager for entertainment were excluded from the world of hardcover novels and "slick paper" magazine fiction by their prohibitive cost, not to mention their often bloodless, self-conscious literary content.

In contrast, the fiction of the all-story pulps featured unfettered imagination, quick-paced narrative and lean, muscular prose. The appeal of the pulps in cost, quantity and vivid storytelling energy was immediate and widespread. In no time, they were a ubiquitous fixture of American life, continuing to increase in number and variety and in the range of stories they published.

To meet the competition, publishers upgraded their products. Street & Smith—the publishing giant that years later would enlist L. Ron Hubbard's

"The Barbarians,"
published in December 1935.

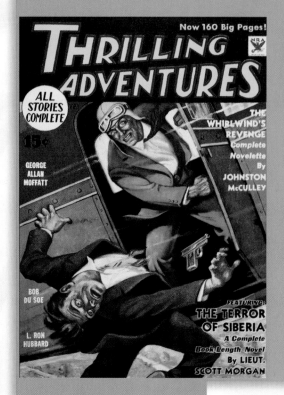

"The Green God"
appeared in this February 1934
issue of *Thrilling Adventures*.

"Yukon Madness,"
first published in August 1935.

"Twenty Fathoms Down,"
published in September 1934.

uniquely versatile literary gifts to revolutionize the science fiction genre—changed *Buffalo Bill* to *Western Story Magazine* and *Nick Carter* to *Detective Story*. New kinds of themes, stories and writing styles emerged—hard-boiled detective, frontier law and order, swords and sorcery, cynically honest private eye, horror and science fiction, among others. Provocatively colorful, irrepressibly popular, these magazines and their content would ultimately influence every later venue of international entertainment, from movies, radio and television to comics, animation and computer video games.

The number and diversity of magazines expanded quickly in the 1920s, enjoying a momentum further bolstered in 1926 when publisher Hugo Gernsback introduced what literary historians generally consider the first "purely" science fiction magazine, *Amazing Stories*. With an emphasis on science over story, however, science fiction started to wane in popularity in the 1930s, only to be revitalized and redefined by L. Ron Hubbard, Robert Heinlein and a handful of other writers in what is still regarded as science fiction's golden age.

Shadowed by the Great Depression and the growing thunder of an approaching world war, broad vistas of imaginative mass entertainment dominated the market in the 1930s, when pulp magazines reached their high watermark in diversity and appeal.

"The Black Sultan,"
published in November 1935.

"Tomb of the Ten Thousand Dead,"
published in October 1936 under the pen name
Capt. Charles Gordon.

Christian's big hands had the native by the shoulders. "Who sent that, you black devil?" he roared.

The Headhunters
by
L. RON HUBBARD

Tom Christian, on a million-dollar trek into the jungle, is trapped by the headhunters and their renegade white leader

Travelers Headed for Trouble

"The Headhunters," published in August 1936. Illustration by Bill Brigham.

"Spy Killer," published in April 1936.

"Hurricane," published in March 1936. Illustration by Bill Brigham.

HURRICANE by L. RON HUBBARD

Captain Spar, escaped from the mire of a penal colony, sets out to get the man who sent him to hell

A moment later a dark, fat face appeared in the lighted crack.

"What you want?"

"I want food. Food, and perhaps information."

"The police have forbidden us to open

so late. Do you wish to cause my arrest?"

"I have money."

The crack opened wider. The mestizo closed and bolted the double door. A half dozen Negroes looked up curiously and then returned to their rum punch.

"Your name is Henri," said the tall man, standing in a puddle of water which oozed out from his shoes.

Henri raised his brows and rubbed his hands, looking up and down the tall one's height. "You know my name? And I know you. You are one they call Captain Spar."

"Yes. Then you got the letter?"

"Yes, I received it. I do not often associate with—convicts."

Captain Spar made no move. "I have money."

His first antagonist was holding a chair high, ready to smash Spar's skull. Spar rolled and fired.

The Man from Hell

HE came through the rain buffeted darkness, slipping silently along a wall, avoiding the triangular patches of light. His stealth was second nature because he had lived with stealth so long. And who knew that death walked with him into the leaden gusts which swept through the streets of Fort de France, Martinique?

He was big, heavy-boned, and he had once weighed more than now. His eyes were silver-gray, almost luminous in the night, like a wolf's. His black hair was plastered down on his forehead, his shirt was dark, soggy with the tempest —and at his waist there gleamed a giant brass buckle. Capless and gaunt, feeling his way through the sullen city, he heard voices issuing from behind a door.

He stopped and then, indecisively, studied the entrance. Finally he rapped.

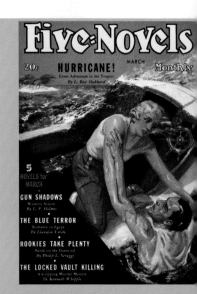

From the first *Argosy* in 1896 to arguably the final issue of *Science Fiction Quarterly* in 1958, the pulps published well over a million stories in upwards of a thousand different magazines—the variety of genre, style, caliber, content and invention without historical parallel. But more than that, the pulps provided a visible, readily accessible forum for many of the country's—and, ultimately, the world's—most gifted and influential writers to seize, ignite and exalt the imagination. Confounding their critics and vindicating the literary loyalties of their legion of readers, the pulps featured the works of writers who remain mainstays of popular fiction to this day, including Dashiell Hammett, Agatha Christie, Raymond Chandler, Erle Stanley Gardner, Sinclair Lewis, Upton Sinclair, Tennessee Williams, Zane Grey, Max Brand, Louis L'Amour, Edgar Rice Burroughs, Robert E. Howard, Isaac Asimov, Ray Bradbury, Robert Heinlein and, of course, L. Ron Hubbard.

From virtually the outset of his literary career, Hubbard ranked among the most productive, versatile and successful writers in popular fiction.

From the beginning, as well, his prodigious output reflected the colorful, Renaissance-man qualities of his life. As with Herman Melville, Mark Twain and Jack London before him, and his contemporary, Ernest Hemingway, Hubbard's experiences and travels—as an explorer and prospector, master mariner and dare-devil pilot, photographer and filmmaker, philosopher and artist, composer and musician, and always, quintessentially, as a writer—found their way into his fiction and into the currents of American culture.

His stories and novels—many of them genre shaping and trendsetting—translated the adventure and wonder of a world-traveler's journeys into living-room entertainment and transformed the exotic and provocative turns of a creative imagination into a compelling literary legacy. As the distinguished author, editor and critic Frederik Pohl has said:

"There are bits and pieces from Ron's work that became part of the language in ways that very few other writers managed. I can still remember scenes from Hubbard's stories when I've forgotten most of the other things I was reading. . . . He had a gift for inventing colorful pictures that still stay with me. . . . Stories with these frequently memorable lines and quotable things. Pictures that stayed in your head."

It is the rare writer who can inscribe lasting impressions upon both the memories of individual readers and the collective consciousness of a culture. The great literary artists who accomplish that feat share a defining ability to shape both the most formidable and the most ordinary of life experiences into literature that appeals to a broad spectrum of the population with authenticity and with themes and perceptions that illuminate and enlarge the human condition.

On Blazing Wings

By L. Ron Hubbard

The city in the sky was full and bright before him, and he was flying into it

"Ron could do more stunts in a sailplane than most pilots can in a pursuit job. He would come out of spins at an altitude of thirty inches and thumb his nose at the undertakers who used to come out to the field and titter."

—Pilot, *July 1934*

Never a detached, armchair spectator, L. Ron Hubbard channeled his intense appetite for adventure and his fierce curiosity about the basic nature of man and Earth's manifold cultures into wide travels throughout his life in pursuit of his own research and to broaden and diversify his education in the classroom of the world. The result has been works of insight and imagination that have outlived both the magazines that popularized his writing and the man himself.

Danger Is My Business

In writing an adventure story a writer has to know that he is adventuring for a lot of people who cannot. The writer has to take them here and there about the globe and show them excitement and love and realism. As long as that writer is living the part of an adventurer when he is hammering the keys, he is succeeding with his story.

"Adventuring is a state of mind. If you adventure through life, you have a good chance to be a success on paper.

"Adventure doesn't mean globe-trotting, exactly, and it doesn't mean great deeds. Adventuring is like art. You have to live it to make it real."

—*L. Ron Hubbard*

One reporter wrote that as a barnstorming flier in the early thirties, L. Ron Hubbard "just dared the ground to come up and hit him."

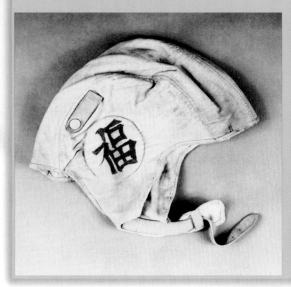

Hubbard's flying helmet bearing the Japanese characters for "Good luck."

Of the over two hundred and fifty novels, novellas and short stories L. Ron Hubbard published in his extraordinary career, nearly a hundred were action and adventure tales. In them are reflections of the author's travels and discoveries, passed through the prism of what the *Portland Journal* called "an inexhaustible imagination." Over the years, Hubbard compiled thousands of diary, ledger and journal pages—essentially his personal notebook of the world—which formed a part of his meticulous research and pursuit of the "slim, forgotten fact" that would elevate a story from the mundane to the memorable. Thus, his action and adventure tales are crafted from personal experience and observation, fortified by devotion to detail, conceived with the reader in mind, and delivered with power and artistry.

"Adventure," Hubbard said, "I well know, is in the heart, not in the view." In his stories, as in his life, he adventured grandly, carrying a multitude of readers, with stunning verisimilitude, into the cold, storm-swept labyrinth of the sea, or the withering heat of a desert vastness, or the dark languors of the jungle, or the wild currents of the upper air—or, in his great speculative adventures of time and space, into the rigors and daring splendors of the long passage between the stars.

EVERY STORY COMPLETE

Five Novels

20c

5 NOVELS for NOVEMBER

Hurtling Wings
Adventure Rides the Air
By L. Ron Hubbard

With Spurs Clashing
A Dramatic Novel of the West
By L. P. Holmes

The Black Box Murder
Fate Unravels a Mystery
By David Whitelaw

Island Drums
A Romance of the South Sea Isles
By Byron Kennedy

The Ostrich Pass
Action Sweeps the Gridiron
By John Murray Reynolds

 The RED by DRAGON
L. RON HUBBARD

"The Phantom Patrol," published in January 1935.
Illustration by Bill Brigham.

EVERY STORY COMPLETE
Five Novels
20c

5 NOVELS for JANUARY

Outlaws' Round-Up
Vengeance Takes the Trail
By C. B. Glasscock

The Phantom Patrol
Adventure with the Coast Guard
By L. Ron Hubbard

Mistress Headlong
Romance in the Hungarian Hills
By F. V. W. Mason

King Coal's Luck
A Stirring Story of the Turf
By Philip L. Scruggs

The Murray Affair
An Exciting Mystery Novel
By Donald G. Cooley

EVERY STORY COMPLETE
Five Novels
20c

5 NOVELS for FEBRUARY

The Red Dragon
Fascinating Adventure in China
By L. Ron Hubbard

Salty Sails
Sport Takes to the Sea
By Philip L. Scruggs

Justice Cracks the Whip
A Vigorous Story of the West
By L. P. Holmes

Murder by Moonlight
Mystery Haunts the Woods
By John Murray Reynolds

When Flood-Waters Roll
The Mississippi Turns Destroyer
By Walter Marquiss

"The Red Dragon," published in February 1935.
Illustration by Bill Brigham.

The PHANTOM

CHAPTER ONE

THE SINKING PLANE

CRISP and brittle, the staccato torrent ripped out from the headphones. "S O S . . . S O S . . . Down in storm twenty miles south of Errol Island. S O S . . . Hull leaking. Starboard wing smashed . . . Cannot last two hours . . . S O S . . . Transport Plane New Orleans bound sinking twenty miles—"

Johnny Trescott's opinion of the matter was amply summed up in a single word, "Damn!"

"Bad news, Chief?" asked Heinie Swartz, above the yelling gale.

Regardless of setting, his adventure stories had the unmistakable ring of authenticity. Whether imperiled by a forbidding storm at sea or prey to the desert's unforgiving expanse, whether the danger came from a jungle or the stratosphere, Hubbard's characters and action seemed genuine. But timeless themes indelibly stamped his adventure tales as well—courage, danger, leadership, honor, love, the bare-knuckle struggle between right and wrong or good and evil. An excellent example of this is his 1937 short story "Red Death Over China," where an American pilot wrestles with blunted idealism and a fundamental moral choice that will define both his life and the lives of others. His dilemma is brought to light by the harsh realities of a nation torn by invasion and civil war, the China Hubbard knew from his journeys and which he recreated with striking color and detail.

Hubbard's adventure stories radiate from pivotal choices—between action and inaction, impulse and restraint, justice and injustice—that are faced by principal and satellite characters alike as they confront relentless adversaries and overwhelming odds. In "Hurtling Wings"—the cover story in the November 1934 issue of the hugely popular all-story adventure magazine *Five Novels Monthly*—a test pilot must deal decisively, but in good conscience, with a competitor who will go to any

This charcoal sketch of a twenty-five-year-old L. Ron Hubbard by friend and artist Richard Albright hung above the editor's desk at *Five Novels Monthly,* one of the pulp era's most popular magazines.

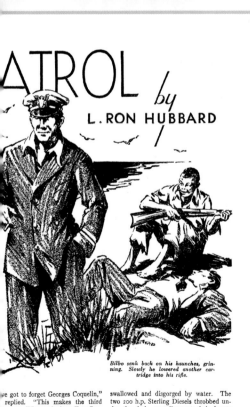

ATROL *by* L. RON HUBBARD

Bilbo sank back on his haunches, grinning. Slowly he lowered another cartridge into his rifle.

ve got to forget Georges Coquelin," replied. "This makes the third a row. Why can't these Two-Con-pilots take care of themselves?" e Swartz eyed the dripping fore-the lunging seventy-five footer. eas topped with froth were break-he one-pound gun was alternately

swallowed and disgorged by water. The two 200 h.p. Sterling Diesels throbbed under the deck, pounding out their hearts against the blow. For five hours the Coast Guard Patrol Boat *1004* had barely held her own.

Heinie turned back to Trescott, noting the wild look in the C.P.O.'s sea-blue eyes.

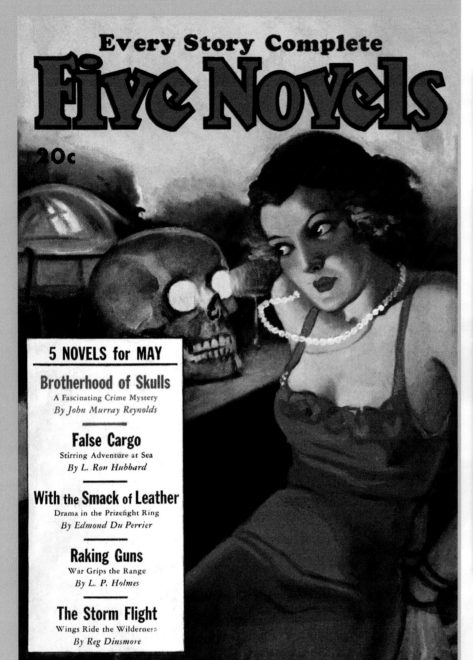

EVERY STORY COMPLETE

Five Novels

20c

5 NOVELS for MAY

Brotherhood of Skulls
A Fascinating Crime Mystery
By John Murray Reynolds

False Cargo
Stirring Adventure at Sea
By L. Ron Hubbard

With the Smack of Leather
Drama in the Prizefight Ring
By Edmond Du Perrier

Raking Guns
War Grips the Range
By L. P. Holmes

The Storm Flight
Wings Ride the Wilderness
By Reg Dinsmore

"False Cargo,"
published in May 1935.

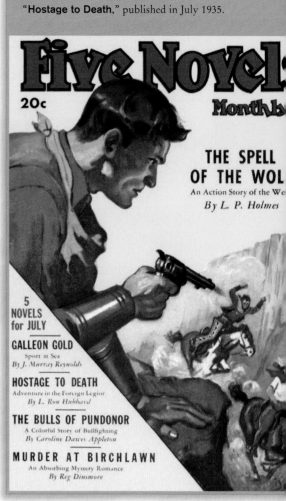

"Hostage to Death," published in July 1935.

Five Novels Monthly

20c

THE SPELL
OF THE WOL
An Action Story of the We
By L. P. Holmes

5
NOVELS
for JULY

GALLEON GOLD
Sport at Sea
By J. Murray Reynolds

HOSTAGE TO DEATH
Adventure in the Foreign Legion
By L. Ron Hubbard

THE BULLS OF PUNDONOR
A Colorful Story of Bullfighting
By Caroline Dawes Appleton

MURDER AT BIRCHLAWN
An Absorbing Mystery Romance
By Reg Dinsmore

lengths, including murder, to win the air-mail contracts they both seek. The story's riveting action and sweep of realism, woven from L. Ron Hubbard's own hands-on experience as a barnstorming pilot, evoked a flurry of reader reactions, few more telling than this:

"What I liked about Hubbard's 'Hurtling Wings' is that it is not one of these cut and dried stories, but [is] full of action. It makes one wish he was going up in the air, riding adventure and thrills, instead of reading it."

Hubbard stories were a regular feature in *Five Novels Monthly*, with thirty-four published between 1934 and 1940. The enthusiasm for his fiction by the magazine and its editor, Florence McChesney, was unmistakable. In one issue, for example, two of the five novels were Hubbard's, one under his own name, the other under a pseudonym. Note McChesney's exuberance when announcing that a

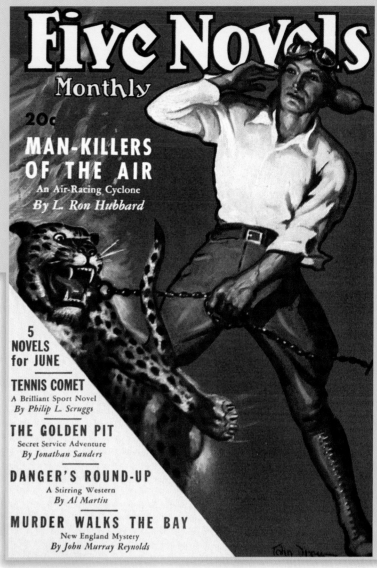

"Man-Killers of the Air," published in June 1935.

Ron and colleague Paul Wilkerson, in a swollen alluvial-bearing river following a tropical storm, during his second Caribbean voyage in 1932, the Puerto Rican Mineralogical Expedition.

Editor's note from the October 1934 issue of *Thrilling Adventures*.

I guess L. Ron Hubbard needs no introduction. From the letters you send in, his yarns are about the most popular we have published. Several of you have wondered, too, how he gets the splendid color which always characterizes his stories of the faraway places.

The answer is, he's been there, brothers. He's been, and seen, and done, and plenty of all three of them!

Editor

"Forbidden Gold," published in October 1935.
Illustrations by Bill Brigham.

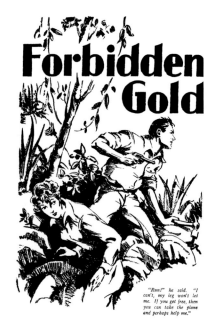

Forbidden Gold

by L Ron Hubbard

With a dead man's hatred challenging him to the impossible,
Kurt Reid stakes his life against the loaded dice of destiny

Dead Man's Trick

"THAT'S all you have to do, Mr. Reid. Just match this gold nugget, and old Nathan Reid's money is yours." Kimmelmeyer fixed a legal eye on Kurt Reid and rolled the nugget in question about in his soft, plump hand. Kurt Reid cocked his head a little on one side and took a long drag at a cigarette. Then he crossed his long legs and exhaled the smoke in a blue cloud, which enveloped the desk. Kimmelmeyer coughed, but his eyes remained very fatherly and legal.

Compared to Kurt, Kimmelmeyer was small. Kimmelmeyer's head was bald. Kimmelmeyer's ears were elfinly pointed. His chin was sunk far down in a wing collar, giving his face a half-moon appearance.

"That's all I have to do!" said Kurt with a twisty grin, "What's the matter, Kimmelmeyer, don't you like me any better than Nathan Reid did?"

"Like you!" gaped Kimmelmeyer, missing the point.

"You act as if I were about to go on a Sunday school picnic instead of a gold hunt in Yucatan. What if I don't want to go?"

The legal look vanished. Kimmelmeyer stared, amazed. He did not feel at all at ease with this young man. Something in Kurt's attitude was vaguely insolent. His poise was too astounding. No, Kimmel-

"Run!" he said. "I can't, my leg won't let me. If you get free, then you can take the plane and perhaps help me."

Five Novels
Monthly
20c

THUNDER IN THE WEST
A Gripping Range Romance
By L. P. Holmes

5 NOVELS for OCTOBER

GRUDGE FIGHT
A Prize-Ring Novel
By Philip L. Scruggs

FORBIDDEN GOLD
Adventure in Yucatan
By L. Ron Hubbard

SIX HOURS TO LIVE
A Detective-Action Story
By Paul Ernst

THE DEVIL'S LAIR
Romantic Adventure in Abyssinia
By Zachary Cook

Bruce whirled about, furious. "Don't stand there like a fool! Spot the direction of their course!"

"They got the machine-guns," protested Sloan, nursing his hand.

"They—they *what?*" stormed Bruce.

"The two machine-guns you said to put in that ship."

"I told you to take them out!" Bruce roared.

"Hang on," he said, and began to lower her over sixty feet of space.

of lead. The rudder slammed hard over, hammered there. The yellow ship careened into a right angle turn.

The dust rising from the skidding tail partially obscured the ship for a moment, but when Connelly saw it again it was flying free, headed up into the wind, wheels turning idly under the past momentum of the ground.

They were gone.

"I tried to, but I was afraid a Customs man would see me or something. Honest to God, Bruce—oh, my hand!"

new L. Ron Hubbard novel, "Trouble on His Wings" (which blends two of the author's passions, flying and photography), would appear as the cover story in the January 1939 issue of *Five Novels:* "This new novel of his hits the top with a bang. It's got everything—speed, excitement, swell characters, a good strong plot and enough thrills in flying adventure to bring a mummy back to life. It's news-camera stuff—flying and picture-taking from the air, to the tune of flaming forests and machine-gun bullets. A five-star air adventure, with Hubbard at his best."

"Five Mex for a Million," published in November 1935.

"Under the Black Ensign," published in August 1935.

Smashing
NOVELS
MAGAZINE

3 Complete Novels

MAY
15¢

A DOUBLE-ACTION MAGAZINE

"OF GUTS AND GUNS"
A Complete Western Novel by
EDGAR L. COOPER

"LOOT OF THE SHANUNG"
Complete Adventure Novel by
L. RON HUBBARD

"BLACK DEATH"
Complete Detective Novel by
PHILIP SHARPE

"Loot of the Shanung,"
published in May 1936.

"Black Towers to Danger,"
published in October 1936.
Illustration by Bill Brigham.

Five-Novels
20¢
Monthly

BLACK TOWERS OF DANGER
Romantic Adventure in Venezuela
By L. Ron Hubbard

5 NOVELS for OCTOBER

NO DECISION!
A Prizefight Novel
By Philip L. Scruggs

THE DEVIL'S SPURS
The Range Fights a Gold Rush
By Al Martin

MURDER BY COMPASS
A Stirring Mystery Novel
By Maurice Beam

THE CURSE OF HI FONG
Adventure among the Malays
By Raoul Dexter

BLACK
to DANGER
by
L. RON HUBBARD

Bill fired. El Opio went down, his arm shattered.

Big Bill, trying to prove his oil well, finds Venezuela a hot spot for trouble

TOWERS

"**Red Death Over China**" was published in this issue of *War Birds* in October 1937.

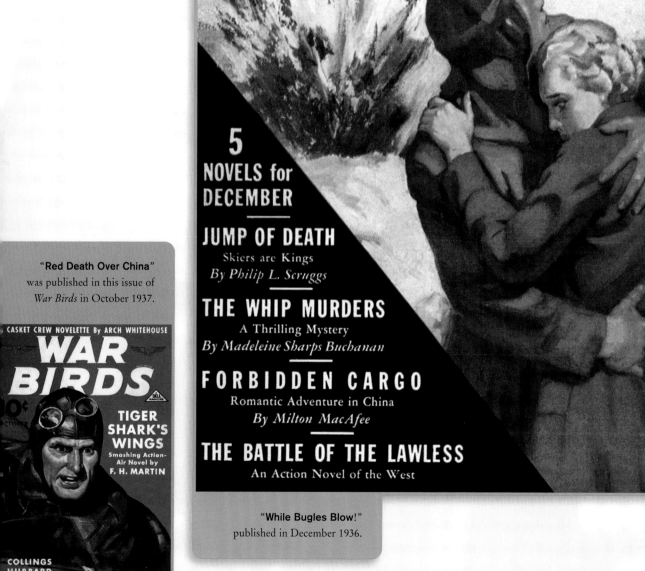

"While Bugles Blow!" published in December 1936.

The Devil with Wings

by L. RON HUBBARD

The most daring, most feared man in China—the white pilot openly challenges China's enemies to battle—with no quarter asked!

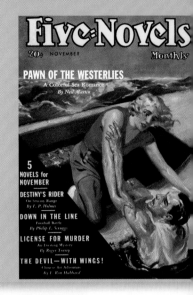

TOKIO, JAPAN—May 9 (Tekko News Agency)—General Ytosho Shimokado, commanding Japanese Imperial Troops at Port Arthur, Manchukuo, announced today that Akuma-no-Hané, infamous white pilot, was killed last week near the Amur River.

Captain Ito Shinohari, famous and gallant figure of the Imperial Japanese Military Intelligence, was credited with the slaying.

Akuma-no-Hané, The Devil With Wings, has long conducted his lawless operations against the Manchukuo government and, it is reported, recently attempted to bring about the overthrow of the Son of Heaven, whose gentle rule of Manchukuo is well known.

It is also rumored that Akuma-no-Hané was in the pay of Russia and played considerable part in instigating the recent clash of arms between Japan and Russia in the unknown reaches of the Amur River.

A will-o-the-wisp figure, the as yet unidentified renegade will long be remembered for his three-year reign of terror.

The details of the slaying have not been reported. It is said that Captain Ito Shinohari will be rewarded with the Order of the Rising Sun.

The Night Marauder

DARKNESS and silence lay like velvet paws upon the Japanese Intelligence Headquarters at Port Arthur. The far-off midnight hum of the

CAPTAIN ITO SHINOHARI
HERO IN KILLING OF
AKUMA-NO-HANÉ

With a slow, overhand motion, Forsythe looped the grenade straight at the hurrying soldiery.

"The Devil — With Wings," published in November 1937.

Five Novels Monthly's October 1938 issue included two L. Ron Hubbard stories—the cover story as well as "Branded Outlaw," published under the pen name Barry Randolph.

"Trouble on His Wings," published in January 1939.

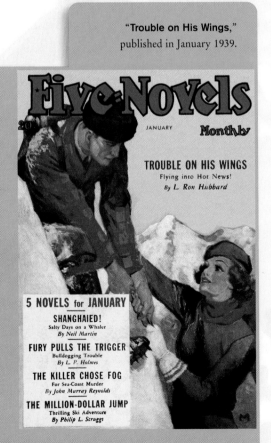

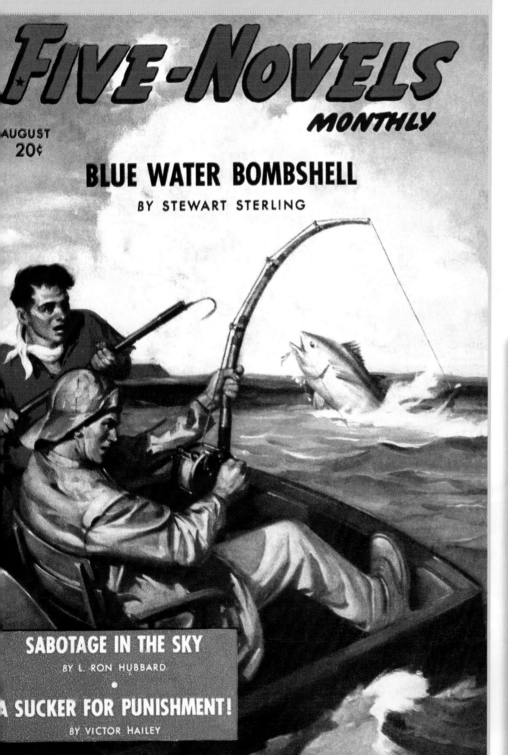

FIVE-NOVELS
MONTHLY

AUGUST
20¢

BLUE WATER BOMBSHELL
BY STEWART STERLING

SABOTAGE IN THE SKY
BY L. RON HUBBARD

A SUCKER FOR PUNISHMENT!
BY VICTOR HAILEY

"Sabotage in the Sky,"
published in August 1940.

"The Falcon Killer," published in April 1939.
Illustration by Bill Brigham.

Five-Novels
Monthly

20¢
APRIL

THE FALCON KILLER
Thrilling Air Adventure
By
L. Ron Hubbard

5 NOVELS for APRIL

GUNSLINGERS' HOLIDAY
A Gripping Western Novel
By Wes Farga

SMASH THROUGH TO GOAL!
Polo Battle
By Philip L. Scruggs

RACKETEERS AT SEA
A Colorful Sea Novel
By David Allan Ross

THE DEVIL'S AT THE DOOR
A Fascinating Mystery
By Stewart Sterling

The
Falcon Killer
By
L. Ron Hubbard

FIRST there had been a city; then there had been bright and hungry flame; now there was nothing but a corpse-gutted ruin where men moved of the Tatars, led by the Scourge of Mankind, but its death had not come from the wastes of the north. Wings in the sky had passed their shadows over the

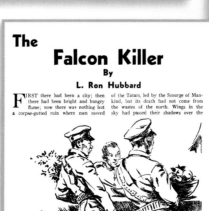

Both Szui Mai and Dmitri stared at Gaylord, wondering whether they should talk

There were many more aviation stories that celebrated what Hubbard once described as the "terrible grandeur" of the skies, in *Five Novels Monthly* and other pulps, among them "Arctic Wings," "Man-Killers of the Air," "Sabotage in the Sky" and "The Lieutenant Takes the Sky." And there were his stories of what he called "drama and high tension" that appeared frequently in other widely read adventure magazines, including *Top-Notch, Thrilling Adventures, Adventure* and *Sky Birds*. Prominent among those tales were "The Chee-Chalker," "While Bugles Blow!" "Starch and Stripes," "Five Mex for a Million," "The Small Boss of Nunaloha" and "Cargo of Coffins," and his carefully researched historical adventure/romances "Under the Black Ensign" and "Mr. Tidwell, Gunner." These and the soon-to-come "Hell Job" stories vaulted L. Ron Hubbard to the forefront of popular adventure fiction and kept him there.

"The Iron Duke," published in July 1940. Illustration by Bill Brigham.

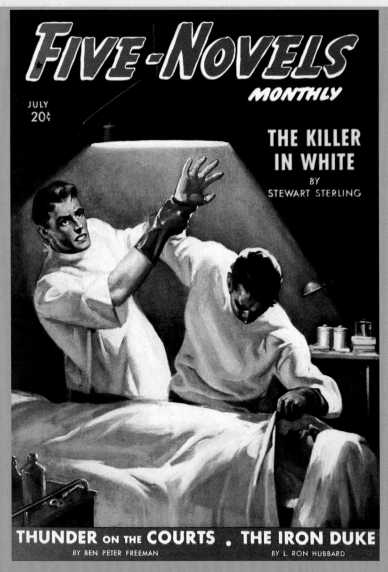

L. RON HUBBARD

But somehow he could not keep the contempt out of his voice, now that he had won. "You will declare the election by the end of the week?"

"Certainly," said Blacky. "Yes—yes, indeed. Now, if I can be shown the way out of this place—"

STUB was wild. He had torn through every inch of the garden and the hotel without once being able to stop and ask anybody any questions, for fear Blacky had been taken by the authorities, who would then, naturally, be desirous of taking Stub as well. And when, at nine-thirty,

The archduke found himself spun about and made into a shield

distrait and on the verge of collapse to the point of needing a drink of anisette, no matter what risks he had to run to win it, he stumbled into the grill *en route* to the bar and found Blacky—

Yes, it was certainly Blacky, sitting there with half a ton of silvery service spread

Article from *Adventure* magazine, October 1935.

Adventure

Vol. 93. No. 5   October 1, 1935   Twice A Month

THE
CAMP-FIRE

*where readers, writers
and adventurers
meet*

L RON HUBBARD *joins our Writers' Brigade with his leatherneck yarn, "He Walked to War." Hubbard is a tall red-haired chap with a service background, his father being an officer. He introduces himself at the Camp-Fire.—Howard V. L. Bloomfield, Editor.*

I was born in Nebraska and three weeks later went to Oklahoma. From there to Missouri, then to Montana. When I was a year old, they say I showed some signs of settling down, but I think this is merely rumor. Changing locales from the Pacific Coast to the Atlantic Coast every few months, it was not until I was almost twelve that I first left the United States. And it was not until I was sixteen that I headed for the China Coast.

In spite of changing schools, I received an education. I have some very poor grade sheets which show that I studied to be a civil engineer in college.

Civil engineering seemed very handsome at the time. I met the lads in their Stetsons from Crabtown to Timbuktu and they seemed to lead a very colorful existence squinting into their transits. However, too late, I was sent up to Maine by the Geological Survey to find the lost Canadian Border. Much bitten by seven kinds of insects, gummed by the muck of swamps, fed on johnny cake[1] and tarheel,[2] I saw instantly that a civil engineer had to stay far too long in far too few places and so I rapidly forgot my calculus and slip stick and began to plot ways and means to avoid the continuance of my education. I decided on an expedition into the Caribbean.

It was a crazy idea at best and I knew it, but I went ahead anyway, chartered a four-masted schooner and embarked with some fifty luckless souls who haven't ceased their cursings yet. Our present generation just doesn't take to salt horse, dried peas, and a couple quarts of water a day.

1. johnny cake: corn bread baked on a griddle.
2. tarheel: thick syrup made of molasses and maple syrup.

But the expedition did the trick. I did not have to return to college. Instead I returned to the West Indies.

I might remark upon a coincidence which has always amazed me. While in the West Indies I discovered signs of gold on an island and, harboring the thought that the conquistadores might have left some gold behind, I determined to find it.

. . . After half a year or more of intensive search, after wearing my palms thin wielding a sample pick, after assaying a few hundred sacks of ore, I came back, a failure.

But a month after my return to Maryland, I discovered a vein of honeycomb quartz in the back pasture. The body of ore was tremendous, the visible vein several yards wide at the narrowest. Under the $20.67[3] an ounce, it assayed $82.34 a ton, and it is now worth about $145 a ton. However, to mine it takes money and I would have to stay close to Maryland. It's still there.

Chronological narration, in this short sketch, is impossible. Therefore, permit me to jump about a bit.

I was once convinced that the future of aviation lies in motorless flight. Accordingly I started gliding and soaring with the rest of the buzzards, and finally succeeded in establishing a record which has no official existence whatever and no reason, indeed,

for existing. I traveled better than eighty miles an hour for twelve minutes in a soaring plane, maintaining the same altitude about an airport which is set on a flat plain. Answer: Heat lift from the circling concrete road.

From there I went into power flight, the high spot of which came on a barnstorming trip through the Midwest in a five-lunged[4] crate which staggered rather than flew. All one summer, I tried very hard to meet St. Pete, but evidently that gentleman either lost my name from the roll or my luck is far better than I think it is.

Unfortunately, in my Asiatic wanderings, no one, not even Hindu fortunetellers, thought to inform me that I would someday make my living with a typewriter and so I completely forgot to conduct myself informatively and devoted my time to enjoying life.

In Peiping, for instance, I did not avail myself of photographic impressions I might well have gained. I completely missed the atmosphere of the city, devoting most of my time to a British major who happened to be head of the Intelligence out there.

In Shanghai, I am ashamed to admit that I did not tour the city or surrounding country as I should have. I know more about 131 Bubbling Wells Road and its wheels[5] than I do about the history of the town.

In Hong Kong . . . well, why take up space?

Time after time, people accuse me of

---

3. The price of an ounce of gold circa 1935.

4. five-lunged: five-cylindered.
5. wheels: reference to wheels of gambling machines, i.e., the roulette wheel.

having been in the Marines. Pushed right up against the wall, I am forced to admit a connection with that very cosmopolitan outfit, however short lived and vague. I was once a top-kicker[6] in the 20th because, as they sing in Shin-ho,[7]

> I walked down the street
> Without a cent in my jeans,
> And that is the reason
> I joined the Marines.

I am not sure that calling squads east and west fits a man for writing, but it does give him a vocabulary.

One thing I might mention in connection with the leathernecks, most of the fiction written about them is of an intensely dramatic type, all do and die and *semper fidelis* and the dear old flag.

To me the Marine Corps is a more go-to-hell outfit than the much-lauded French Foreign Legion ever could be. The two are comparable in many ways. God knows what you'll find in either, from college professors to bellhops. Just why the disappointed lover has to sneak off for North Africa all the time is a riddle. More men have taken refuge in the Corps than in the Legion and, judging from association, leathernecks certainly lead a sufficiently exciting existence.

I've known the Corps from Quantico to Peiping, from the South Pacific to the West Indies, and I've never seen any flag-waving. The most refreshing part of the USMC is that they get their orders and start out and do the job and that's that. Whether that job was to storm the heights of Chapultepec so that the United States Army could proceed, or to dislodge a crazy gentleman named John Brown from an arsenal at Harpers Ferry, or to knock off a few Boxers for the glory of England, your Marine went and did the job and then retired to bind up his wounds while everyone else went on parade.

Let it suffice. This is more than a thumbnail sketch, but I hope it's a passport to your interest. I know a lot of you out there, and I haven't heard from you in years. I know I haven't had any address, but I'm certain the editor will forward my mail.

When I get back from Central America, where I'm going soon, I'll have another yarn to tell.

L. Ron Hubbard

---

6. top-kicker: first sergeant; drill sergeant.
7. Shin-ho: town in northern Japan.

THE "HELL JOB" SERIES

L. Ron Hubbard had already achieved popular fiction prominence when, in 1936, he proposed a sequence of stories based on the world's "extra-hazardous" occupations to the editor of *Argosy*, the oldest, most enduring and perhaps the most celebrated of the pulp fiction magazines. The idea, which was accompanied by the initial manuscripts, was to produce a series of action stories, each focusing on one of the most dangerous jobs in the world—like steeplejack, test pilot and wild-animal trainer. In other words, the jobs that underwriters refused to insure.

Hubbard's stature as a writer of unusual ability was already broadly established, though he was still only twenty-five and had published his first story just two years earlier. He had been elected president of the New York Chapter of the American Fiction Guild, whose membership included Dashiell Hammett, Raymond Chandler and Edgar Rice Burroughs, among others, and he was much in demand by pulp magazines of every description.

Now, in a publication that gave a mainstream voice to writers like Burroughs (Tarzan), C. S. Forester (Hornblower) and Robert E. Howard (Conan), and was often closed to first-tier writers even after years of trying, Hubbard was given the go-ahead to research and write no fewer than fifteen adventure stories. But with the flower came the thorns. There would be unremitting deadlines imposed and enforced by a taskmaster editor, Jack Byrne, who vowed to make the "Hell Job" series "the biggest thing in *Argosy*."

Hubbard met the challenges and surpassed them. He brought to the series the range of his creative skills, the breadth of his own exploits as a pilot and navigator, helmsman and explorer, spelunker and prospector, and a gift for both scholarly and empirical research. "If you are going to write a story about logging," he once said, "well, you'd better get in and log, man."

L. Ron Hubbard in Puerto Rico during his West Indies Mineralogical Expedition in 1932—one of the two Caribbean expeditions he organized and led that year.

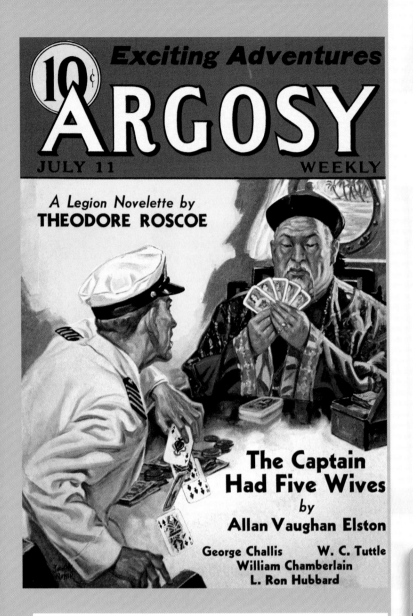

Exciting Adventures

10¢

ARGOSY

JULY 11 **WEEKLY**

A Legion Novelette by
THEODORE ROSCOE

The Captain Had Five Wives
by
Allan Vaughan Elston

George Challis   W. C. Tuttle
William Chamberlain
L. Ron Hubbard

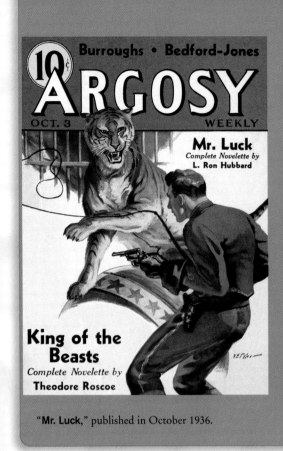

Burroughs • Bedford-Jones

10¢

ARGOSY

OCT. 3 **WEEKLY**

Mr. Luck
Complete Novelette by
L. Ron Hubbard

King of the Beasts
Complete Novelette by
Theodore Roscoe

"**Mr. Luck,**" published in October 1936.

Sleepy McGee
By
L. RON HUBBARD

We jerked him up and out

Only the laziest man in the world could build a road through ten miles of rain-soaked jungle!

The first of the "**Hell Job**" series, "**Sleepy McGee,**" appeared in this issue, July 11, 1936.

The story "**Deep-Sea Diver**" appeared in this October 1936 issue.

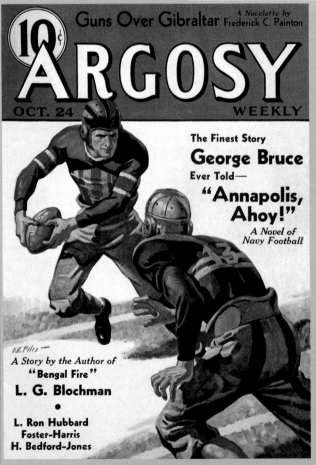

Guns Over Gibraltar *A Novelette by* Frederick C. Painton

10¢

ARGOSY

OCT. 24 **WEEKLY**

The Finest Story
George Bruce
Ever Told—
"**Annapolis, Ahoy!**"
A Novel of Navy Football

A Story by the Author of
"*Bengal Fire*"
L. G. Blochman
•
L. Ron Hubbard
Foster-Harris
H. Bedford-Jones

That meant experiencing the "hell jobs" for himself. That meant diving into the chill waters of Puget Sound in one of the cumbersome deep-sea diving suits of the period and venturing out on the girders of a New York skyscraper with a steeplejack. And that meant drawing on the personal hazards of his earlier Caribbean and South Pacific journeys, from a Puerto Rican mine cave-in and the perils of building a road through the jungles of Guam to his ascent of Mount Pelée, a live volcano on the island of Martinique.

Illustration for "**The Big Cats**," published October 1936 in *Argosy*.

The Ethnologist

By L. RON HUBBARD
Author of "River Driver," "Mr. Luck," etc.

Reading a dusty book, or outwitching witch doctors in the midst of a fear-crazed jungle tribe—it's all in the day's work for a good ethnologist

They were weaving about a great fire

Rosie thundered down upon him

The Big Cats

By L. RON HUBBARD

What treacherous beast of the big top stalked outside the bars, more deadly than the snarling tiger who raged inside the cage?

Illustration from "**The Ethnologist**," published in November 1936 in *Argosy*.

The "Hell Job" series debuted in the July 11, 1936, issue of *Argosy* with "Sleepy McGee," a richly detailed story about the dangers and frustrations of building a road through a Pacific Island jungle at the height of the monsoon season. The series then progressed, as often as weekly to meet reader demand, through "Don't Rush Me," "Mr. Luck," "Test Pilot," "Deep-Sea Diver," "The Big Cats," "River Driver," "The Ethnologist," "Mine Inspector," "The Shooter," "Steeplejack," "Flying Trapeze," "Mountaineer" and "A Lesson in Lightning" to the final story, "Nine Lives," in the August 21, 1937, issue of the magazine.

To this day, the "Hell Job" stories retain their verve, dramatic intensity and signature Hubbard authenticity. And they still impart the insights that so appealed to *Argosy*'s large readership when they first appeared. Now, reading them newly, Richard Kyle, the current editor of *Argosy*, sees a larger dimension in the stories as well:

"L. Ron Hubbard was only twenty-five when he wrote the Hell Job stories about the most dangerous professions a man can put his hand to and it was evident in each of them that he had done his research by living those jobs himself or finding out from the men who did.

"Whatever the Hell Job, every detail rings true.

"But what is extraordinary about these stories is that the characters are authentic, too. Somehow Ron knew things that twenty-five-year-olds weren't supposed to know—how men thought, what was in their hearts and the goals they fought for. And he knew the time when you had to take a beating if you were going to win out in the end.

"And he knew how cold it is on the mountain, inside a man as well as out."

The "Hell Job" stories are *Argosy* landmarks that amplified already well established reputations of both the magazine and the author. They also made L. Ron Hubbard one of the most sought-after adventure writers of his generation. Beyond that, they offered the perfect platform for the 1937 publication of his watershed adventure novel of the early American Northwest, *Buckskin Brigades,* and provided the impetus for the editorial executives of Street & Smith, the world's leading pulp publisher, to bring Hubbard on board to invigorate their newly minted magazine, *Astounding Science Fiction.*

But Hubbard was always multidimensional. While adventure was the first genre he conquered, and science fiction preeminence was still in his future, he was making his mark in other fields as well.

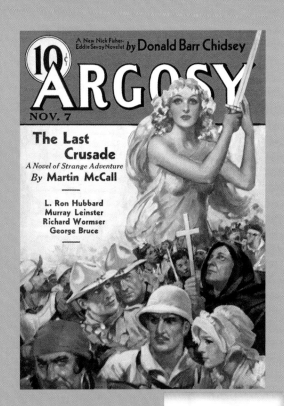

Tiny slammed him down again

River Driver

By L. RON HUBBARD

Author of "Steeple-jack," "Test Pilot," etc.

One million dollars was the prize if the soft-fingered son of roughneck Old Man Planket could go into the woods and kill Johnny Newcome

Ron, circa 1933, on one of the many adventures that he drew from for his famed "**Hell Job**" series.

Horace Purdy Potts' father had always wanted a rugged son, and he got— Horace Purdy Potts. And though the worm may turn, it sometimes needs a push—as Horace found out in the flaming hold of a Caribbee tramp!

Horace bounced off the dock when Captain Brent poked him

A Lesson in Lightning

By L. RON HUBBARD
Author of "Flying Trapeze," "Mountaineer," etc.

Complete
Novelette

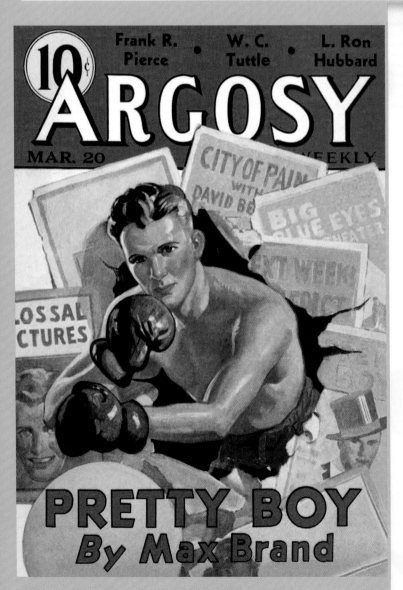

"A Lesson in Lightning" appeared in this March 1937 issue.

ROLLING THE WORDAGE

L. Ron Hubbard's output as a writer was legendary, and the envy of his peers. For years, in the 1930s and 1940s, he regularly produced about one hundred thousand words a month, for the most part working only three hours a day, three days a week. For just the six years between 1934 and 1940 he published an average of a story and a half every two weeks—more than 138 short stories, novelettes and novels in all.

And he wrote fast! If an editor needed a story on a Monday, according to Standard Magazines' editor Jack Schiff, one only had to telephone Ron on Friday.

Even his typewriter gained renown, as science fiction editor and historian Sam Moskowitz pointed out: "Back in the late '30s and '40s there used to be articles in the writer's magazines about the incredible speed with which L. Ron Hubbard wrote. And in those days an electric typewriter was a novelty. Very few writers had one. And the very fact that L. Ron Hubbard had bought an electric typewriter so he could write faster was considered quite newsworthy. Every time one wrote about Hubbard, they would mention his typewriter."

Astounding Science Fiction editor John W. Campbell, Jr., also mentions the typewriter when discussing Hubbard's speed and his techniques: "I've seen L. Ron Hubbard applying all the skilled tricks of the trade, changing rhythm and pace, while typing on his electric typewriter at a pace of some three thousand to four thousand words an hour. When Hubbard has to rewrite a passage, he will start a couple of pages earlier, and gather momentum, so to speak, so that when he hits the revision, he's rolling at his usual high-speed pace. Not only is he not using those techniques of the good author by carefully studied application, he can't make them work if he slows down."

Finally there's Robert A. Heinlein, who tells how he gave a dinner party where he first met Hubbard (who would become a lifelong friend). Campbell was there as well and Hubbard was talking, outlining a fiction story. Campbell suggested he write it and Hubbard said he might. Campbell didn't believe him, saying, "No, I know you. Once you've talked out a story you're through with it. You won't bother with it."

Heinlein explained what happened next. "Well, Ron had to catch a midnight train for Chicago (and then on to Seattle) and he left my apartment, which was practically adjacent to Pennsylvania Station, carrying his typewriter with him. He mailed back the first half [of the story] from Chicago and the second half from Seattle."

Hubbard's productivity involved another amazing statistic: Once established, more than 93 percent of everything he wrote was accepted first draft on the first submission. Nor did he slow down with age. In a twenty-one-month period in 1980–81 he wrote *Battlefield Earth* and *Mission Earth*, along with the two screenplays *Ai! Pedrito!* and *A Very Strange Trip*. These totaled almost two million words.

The last of the **"Hell Job"** series, **"Nine Lives,"** appeared in this August 1937 issue.

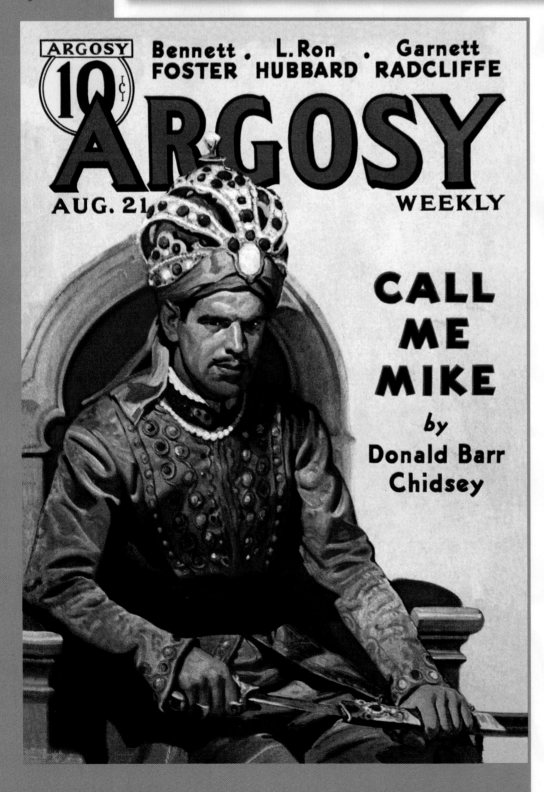

ARGOSY
10¢

Bennett . L. Ron . Garnett
FOSTER HUBBARD RADCLIFFE

ARGOSY

AUG. 21, WEEKLY

CALL ME MIKE

by Donald Barr Chidsey

CRIME DOESN'T PAY

Lon Hubbard's stories of mystery, detection and investigative procedure—the crime-solving processes he once characterized as "the art of observation"—were exceedingly well wrought, if not numerous, and warmly received from their initial appearance in 1934. Fashioned with Hubbard's fast, spare, vivid style, they plunge the reader into the heart of the action, the inside circle of danger within the maze of crime, always with the delineating sense of reality that epitomized Hubbard's fiction, whatever the genre.

With mystery, as with adventure, he refused to write in a vacuum or to speculate about what could be known. Hubbard would not attempt a story without a working knowledge of his subject or an animating perception crafted from firsthand experience or systematic research. To create an authentic foundation for his detective fiction, he interviewed a wide spectrum of law enforcement officials, police officers and federal investigators. Moving to New York City, the hub of the publishing industry, late in 1934, he struck up a long-term friendship with the city's chief medical examiner, who, Hubbard subsequently recalled, introduced him to the fascinating realities of forensic medicine. "The morgue," the coroner assured him, "is open to you anytime, Hubbard." Later, as the youngest-ever president of the New York Chapter of the American Fiction Guild, to promote more accurate use of factual detail in detective and mystery fiction, Hubbard invited the coroner to share his professional expertise with Guild members over lunch. "They would," Ron recounted afterward, "go away from the luncheon the weirdest shades of green." Similar invitations were also extended to other experts, such as the city's highly regarded police commissioner, Lewis J. Valentine. Meanwhile, Hubbard continued to enlarge his range of study, paying a visit to the state correctional facility at Ossining, New York—the notorious Sing Sing—and, in the late 1940s, becoming a special officer with the Los Angeles Police Department.

"**Dead Men Kill**," published in July 1934.

L. Ron Hubbard, center, as president of the New York Chapter of the American Fiction Guild in 1936. The Guild's membership included Dashiell Hammett, Raymond Chandler and Edgar Rice Burroughs.

MOUTHPIECE

Carefully sighting on the first number of the license plate, Mat pulled the trigger

Mat Lawrence Plunges into Some Fast Action in this Breath-Taking Story As He Strives to Track Down the Murderer of His Father

By L. RON HUBBARD

Author of "The Green God," "Calling Squad Cars!" etc.

I T had been a long time since Mat Lawrence had stood upon the corner of a city street; and he found that the sound of traffic— that nerve-tearing clamor of bells, horns, motors, and flat-wheeled street cars—was a foreign and intolerable thing. For three years he had worked on a silent desert building a mammoth power dam. The loudest noise had been a coyote's howl at midnight and the swiftest movement that of a buzzard a mile in the air.

With his usual self-sufficiency he did not know that his dusty boots and battered Stetson made him conspicuous; he only remarked to himself that it was strange how pale the people of his former city had

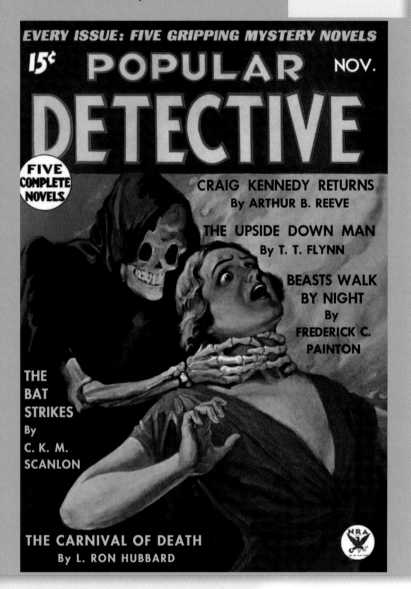

Labyrinth of Shadowed Crimes and Nameless Horrors!

This richly diverse palette of personal experience and untiring inquiry enriched his vastly popular detective and mystery fiction for pulp magazines such as *Phantom Detective, Popular Detective, Mystery Novels* and *Detective Fiction Weekly* and gave his novels and stories an unmistakable cachet of realism.

L. Ron Hubbard's detective fiction tales are not intricately layered, puzzles-within-a-puzzle stories with bizarrely eccentric investigators. Instead they are taut, sharp-edged crime stories with ambiguous clues and the pursuit of an uncertain truth by principled men and women who are, themselves, in harm's way. His first police story, "Calling Squad Cars!"—his second commercially published story—appeared in the April 1934 issue of *Phantom Detective,* one of the genre's premier magazines, and chronicled the career of a suspect police dispatcher. His last detective story, even as he was producing such influential science fiction works as *Ole Doc Methuselah* and the apocalyptic *The End Is Not Yet,* was "Killer's Law," featuring a Nevada sheriff in Washington, D.C., trailing a senator's murderer through the September 1947 pages of *New Detective*.

In those thirteen years, L. Ron Hubbard created some of the era's most memorable crime stories. "Dead Men Kill," which appeared in *Thrilling Detective* in 1934, followed a detective and coroner trying to solve a series of crimes apparently committed by men who had already died. Hubbard enriched "Dead Men Kill" with a glimpse of the voodoo culture he encountered during his West Indies odyssey two years earlier, adding an uncommon flavor to a genre that was one of the pulps' staple formulas. Another notable Hubbard detective yarn, "Brass Keys to Murder," appeared in the April 1935 *Five Novels Monthly* under the pen name of Michael Keith. "Brass Keys" thus made Hubbard a double-barreled threat in *Five Novels,* having already established himself as a front-cover standard-bearer for his adventure stories.

He also let his imagination run wild in his detective fiction. For example, in "The Mad Dog Murder" (*Detective Fiction Weekly,* June 1936), mystery and whimsy came together in a story about a Pekinese suspected of foul play. Three months later, the same magazine published "The Slickers," about an out-of-his-element Texas sheriff in New York City. As he had earlier in "Killer's Law," Hubbard made east and west collide, foreshadowing a major television series about a western sheriff in New York City that aired decades later.

Then there is Hubbard's extraordinary "Death Flyer," his earliest blending of mystery and the supernatural. In this superbly crafted story, a runaway passenger train speeds forever from the past into the future, racing toward an unknowable destiny. The closing lines of the story memorably encapsulate its strange, haunted mood, evoked from the point of view of a civil engineer at an abandoned rail site and what had begun as a mundane project:

"A voice seemed to whisper in his ear, 'I will be waiting . . . on the other side. The next time we'll get through.'

"He looked about him, startled, but his survey crew was silent, waiting for him to go on.

"He stepped off down the uneven trail and vanished silently in the twilight of the woods."

"The Death Flyer" still holds the same breathless intensity and unremitting suspense today that it did more than six decades ago, in the April 1936 issue of *Mystery Novels Magazine*.

"Brass Keys to Murder," published in April 1935 under the pen name Michael Keith. Illustration by Bill Brigham.

5 NOVELS for APRIL

Thunder in Warpaint Pass
An Action Novel of the West
By Al Martin

The Singing Slugger
Battle on the Baseball Diamond
By Philip L. Scruggs

Mesa of Lawless Guns
A Stirring Story of the Range
By L. P. Holmes

Brass Keys to Murder
Mystery Strikes the Waterfront
By Michael Keith

With Swords Unsheathed
A Colorful Adventure-Romance
By Victor Rousseau

"Killer Ape," published in June 1938.

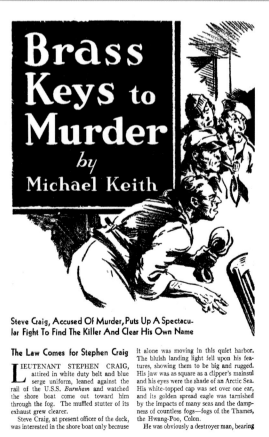

Brass Keys to Murder
by Michael Keith

Steve Craig, Accused Of Murder, Puts Up A Spectacular Fight To Find The Killer And Clear His Own Name

The Law Comes for Stephen Craig

LIEUTENANT STEPHEN CRAIG, attired in white duty belt and blue serge uniform, leaned against the rail of the U.S.S. *Burnham* and watched the shore boat come out toward him through the fog. The muffled stutter of its exhaust grew clearer.

Steve Craig, at present officer of the deck, was interested in the shore boat only because it alone was moving in this quiet harbor. The bluish landing light fell upon his features, showing them to be big and rugged. His jaw was as square as a clipper's mainsail and his eyes were the shade of an Arctic Sea. His white-topped cap was set over one ear, and its golden spread eagle was tarnished by the impacts of many seas and the dampness of countless fogs—fogs of the Thames, the Hwang-Poo, Colon.

He was obviously a destroyer man, bearing

Sailors and longshoremen crowded into the room, their eyes eager with the prospect of a fight.

the stamp of lurching, giddy decks, smashing waves, and full speed ahead.

The shore boat, a chunky affair, rapped against the landing stage, bobbing in the gentle, greasy swell. A man dressed in dirty dungarees held the lines and tried to aid the person who stepped out.

Steve Craig's brows lifted in surprise. A girl had bridged the gap and her high-heeled slippers were pounding up the spotless ladder toward the deck. She glanced

"The Slickers," published in this September 1936 issue.

THE OLD WEST COMES ALIVE

Among the most popular of pulp fiction's genres, the western offered L. Ron Hubbard a made-to-order literary platform. Few, if any, of his contemporaries could invoke the natural authenticity of a Hubbard western because, to him, the western frontier was home.

Hubbard loved the West and understood the tradition and spirit of the frontier that had ever infused the daily life of his Montana childhood. The color, tempo and abundant textures of the formidable land and its rugged dwellers were part of his upbringing and forever part of his creative life. Indeed, his Montana was a microcosm of the western frontier, an immense natural expanse that "swallows men up rather easily," and a place he treasured, in retrospect, for "its do-and-dare attitudes, its wry humor, cowboy pranks, and make-nothing of the worst and most dangerous."

The vast mountains and limitless vistas of the frontier were not merely creatures of his imagination, although he endowed them with the richness of his creative spark. They were where he rode mustangs and range broncs at the age of three and a half, using a cut-down cavalry saddle, "the skirts of which had to be amputated so as to get the doghouse stirrups high enough for me to reach them."

Nor did he just invent colorful frontier characters—he recreated them, styled to be as authentic as the frontier folk he remembered from his youth. "I grew up with old frontiersmen," he recalled, "[with] cowboys, and had an Indian medicine man as one of my best friends." A young Ron Hubbard was made a blood brother of the Blackfeet Indians, panned for gold and traveled across open country that was harsh and imposing, even as the frontier was yielding to the twentieth century and the encroachment of what was referred to as civilization.

But Hubbard's familiarity with the West went well beyond childhood adventures. He was also a dedicated student of the folklore and folkways of range riders and homesteaders, of Indian tribes and their turbulent pasts, of frontier towns and of the people who had crossed a continent to build them, and of the legends that lingered around them long after the original settlers were gone.

His fascination with the frontier and his immersion in its history and culture were the foundation for thirty-eight taut tales of the American West that appeared

Growing up in the rugged country of a still-pioneer Montana, Ron was riding horses by the time he was three.

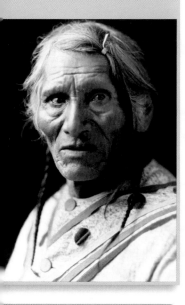

"**Old Tom,**" the Blackfoot Indian medicine man who introduced Ron to their tribal customs and conferred on his young friend the rare status of Blood Brother.

Buckskin Brigades later appeared in *Complete Northwest,* October 1938. Paperback editions were published in 1987 and 1998.

Buckskin Brigades,
first published in 1937.

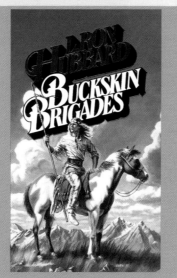

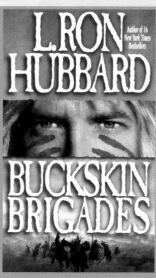

ALL Western MAGAZINE

DELL MAGAZINE

130 Pages For 10¢

MARCH

CATTLE KING FOR A DAY

A THRILLING ACTION NOVEL
By
L. RON HUBBARD

JAMES P. OLSEN
HAPSBURG LIEBE
FOSTER-HARRIS
PHIL SHARPE
And Others!

"Cattle King for a Day,"
published in March 1937.

"Hot Lead Payoff," published in
four parts in the June and July 1938
issues of *Western Story Magazine*.

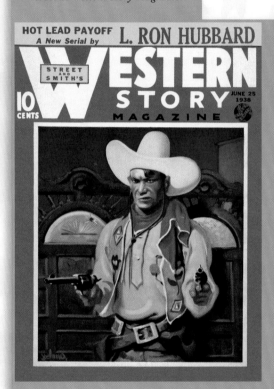

"Under the Die-Hard Brand,"
published in March 1938.

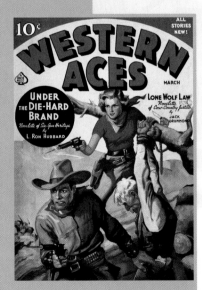

BEGINNING A NEW SERIAL

Hot Lead Payo

By L. RON HUBBARD

Author of "The Toughest Ranger," etc.

in virtually every pulp magazine of consequence for the better part of two decades. To this immensely popular genre, Hubbard brought his firsthand experience with fast rivers and sculptured canyons and his keen understanding of lawmen, desperadoes, prospectors, embattled ranchers and enterprising rustlers. He also shared his appreciation of the vast reaches of land and sky and the majesty of wild horses and of the great predatory cats. Most of all, however, Hubbard captured the persona of a dawning nation in the shifting crosscurrents of history.

In 1937, his true gift for western fiction also resulted in his first published hardcover novel, *Buckskin Brigades*. A towering adventure of the nascent American Northwest, the novel skillfully weaves together the history of the Lewis and Clark Expedition, its encounter with the Blackfeet Indians in 1806 near what is now Helena, Montana, the era's rapacious fur traders, and a figure of singular destiny, a white man named Michael Kirk but known to the Blackfeet as "Yellow Hair." A landmark work for its wealth of scrupulous historical detail and its unconventionally sympathetic portrayal of Indian life and mores, *Buckskin Brigades* is a "western"—but only in the same epic sense that Jack London's *White Fang* is an animal story or Herman Melville's *Moby Dick* is a tale of the sea.

There was an irony to Hubbard's western fiction career. "My first western stories," he later reflected, "were scornfully rejected since they were 'not authentic,' having been written by someone who had been west of Hoboken." His sentiments were echoed elsewhere—by one critic, for example, who deplored the general state of pulp westerns as "cowboy stories written by Manhattan bellhops."

Ron's historical western adventure *Buckskin Brigades* was one of the first novels to present a sympathetically accurate view of the Blackfeet Indians and tribal life mores.

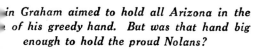

in Graham aimed to hold all Arizona in the of his greedy hand. But was that hand big enough to hold the proud Nolans?

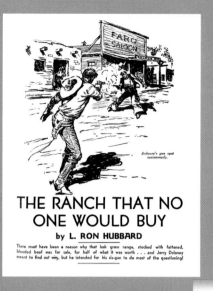

"**The Ranch That No One Would Buy**," published in October 1939.

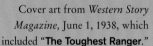

Cover art from *Western Story Magazine*, June 1, 1938, which included "**The Toughest Ranger.**"

Whatever the initial resistance to Hubbard's western fiction, it proved to be brief and inconsequential. Within a year, spurred by their narrative power and genuine authenticity, his western stories began to appear under his own name and under such pen names as Barry Randolph and Ken Martin and later Winchester Remington Colt.

By 1938, the year after the release of *Buckskin Brigades* to critical and popular acclaim, Hubbard's prodigiously versatile output included aviation, adventure and detective fiction. That year also marked the publication of his first two science fiction stories—"The Dangerous Dimension" and "The Tramp." And there were sixteen westerns in 1938 as well, many of them cover features, all of them tight, hard-hitting, trademark Hubbard yarns.

Among the most noteworthy were "Six Gun Caballero" and the four-part "Hot Lead Payoff"—both of which appeared in Street & Smith's *Western Story*. That same year saw the publication of the whimsically engaging "When Gilhooly Was in Flower," which he wrote under the name of Barry Randolph for *Romantic Range,* and the powerful "Empty Saddles" in *Adventure Yarns.* One memorable 1938 issue of *Five Novels Monthly* featured both Barry Randolph's "Branded Outlaw" and L. Ron Hubbard's "The Lieutenant Takes the Sky," an unusual literary double-header.

Ron wrote other notable westerns, of course—"The No-Gun Gunhawk" (1936), whose horseman sent dust "rolling up in a great yellow fog toward the blue"; the memorable "Guns of Mark Jardine" (1949); "Hoss Tamer" (1950), which later aired on NBC's celebrated *Tales of Wells Fargo* television series; and "Shadows From Boot Hill" (1940), his only western fantasy, with these foreboding closing lines:

"His hands clutched meaningless scoops of hot, gritty sand and the world began to tip crazily. . . .

"His own shadow—

"His own shadow—

"Was gone."

An action novelet by
L. RON HUBBARD

As the horses bolted, Old Laramie came to an uneasy landing in the sage and sand

With an Aztec snake whip as his lucky charm,
Old Laramie works miracles for the Lazy G—but when the
smoke clears away he gets the real lowdown!

THE *Magic* QUIRT

CHAPTER I

Grateful Aztec

LOUDLY the voice of the irritated cook rang out. "Git up, there, you Mac! Gieup, Bessie! Carnsarn ye for a pair of busted down, wall-eyed, spavined ignorantipedes! Gettin' so a man can't even git ten winks on his own chuckwagon without you buzzard baits clownin' up!"

Old Laramie curled twenty feet of whip into a powerful pop about their ears and the pair of swaybacks began to pull once more. The chuckwagon clattered and rolled over the last small hump and started down the curving, treacherous trail which led into and through Daly Canyon.

A horse is often wiser than a preoccupied man and Bessie or Mac might have had something to say if they could have talked. For two wagons wouldn't pass on this narrow, precipitous trail. They let the whip pop away their caution and downward they shuffled.

Old Laramie had not liked being disturbed. It was just about dusk and shortly he would be elbow deep in the

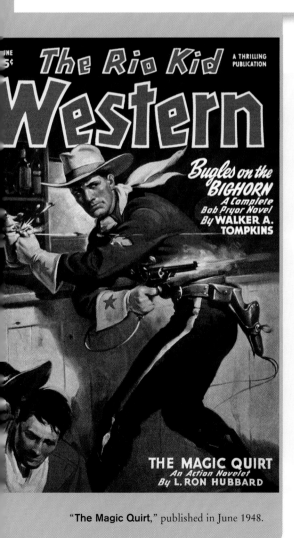

"The Magic Quirt," published in June 1948.

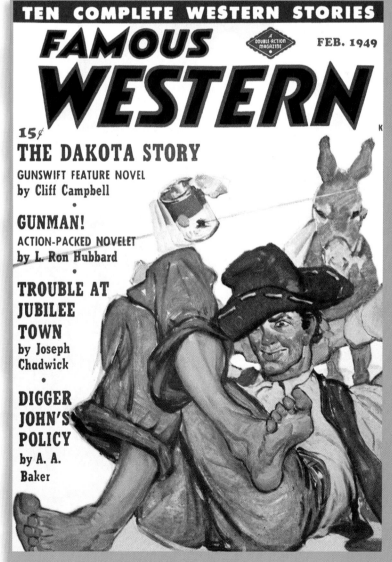

"Gunman!"
published in February 1949.

"Guns of Mark Jardine,"
published in September 1949.

"Gun Boss of Tumbleweed,"
published in April 1949.

Trigger-Quick New
Book-Length Novel
by L. RON HUBBARD

*Mark Jardine and the guns he wore had both become legend
within his lifetime, and Ben Carmody saw a way to use this
legend. But he didn't give Jardine quite enough credit for brains
as well as for fighting ability when he rigged up a boothill trap
for a shooting fool!*

HE HAD NOT come here for trouble; in his thirty years he had had enough of that. He had ridden a long, long ways, a dry and dusty thousand miles from Texas, and he was within an hour of his journey's end. He had hoped to make it all the way without trouble and yet here it was.

He sat tall in his saddle and looked at the stage in the middle of the roaring ford. The water was boiling across the shallows of the freshet swollen stream, purling white through the wheels of the Concord, foaming around the legs of the four-horse team. On the far bank were three men, mounted, just emerged from the alders, and in the hands of one a Henry smoked. It was that report which had stopped Mark Jardine within a yard of riding into view on the bank across from them.

The Concord was trembling as the water tore at it. The restive horses stood only because the bank was barred; their reins were slack and trailing in the current. And, arms and head flopped down from the box, lay the driver, face blown half away.

The man who carried the Henry waved his companions forward. He was an unshaven, dirty man, remarkable for the amount of soiled finery he wore. He had no forehead worth

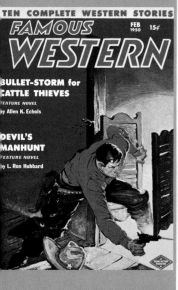

"Devil's Manhunt,"
published in February 1950.

"The No-Gun Man,"
published in May 1950.

A CHAT WITH
THE RANGE BOSS

Here's the low-down on L. Ron Hubbard, whose "Shadows From Boothill" appears in this issue. His literary and other achievements make him blush modestly not only to the roots of his hair but clear out to the end of it.

Dear Range Boss:

Two towns argue about my birth. Tilden, Nebr., says I was born in Lincoln, Nebr.— and Lincoln says I was born in Tilden. I left those parts at the age of three weeks because grandpappy sold out in Nebraska (it was getting too tame) and got himself a spread in Oklahoma. Then it got too tame there and when I was two, I was hauled off to Kalispell, Montana. Because my folks disapproved of the way I walked they glued me to a McClellan saddle and there I stuck unto the age of seven.

My dad, however, being an officer in the navy, didn't like the idea of a bowlegged sailor. So he took me to sea; they say I'd traveled a quarter of a million miles at the age of nineteen.

Got tired of life when very young and took up flying. An old article about me in *The Pilot* says: ". . . The undertakers used to come down to the field and titter." Barnstormed the West and then left wings in favor of sails.

This spring's issue of the *Explorer's Journal* says: "Mr. Hubbard is essentially a writer, but as a trained engineer has done important field work. In 1932-33 he conducted a West Indies Minerals Survey, making a complete mineralogical survey of Puerto Rico. He also directed a motion picture expedition to the West Indies for submarine movies—at the same time obtaining important data for the Government Hydrographic Office. More recently he has been interested in adding to the knowledge of unfrequented passages and islands of the Northwest coast, U.S.A."

Somehow I got started in the writing business. Leaned on my experiences in the West, Asia, the Caribbean, as a pilot, sailor and— *calf-roper*! By some fluke, when I started I fanned out a story a day for six weeks and have since sold all but two. This, of course, spoiled me. Since then I haven't done a tap of *work*—I just *write* which, as everybody knows (har-har!) isn't really work. Four million of my words have been published in fifty-five different magazines. Various moom pitchers have been filmed from my fiction, too. Just now I'm larruping fantasy fiction more than anything else, though I've been writing Westerns for some time too.

Hope your readers like "Shadows From Boothill." Truth is that the old West was superstitious in the extreme and Injun lore reeks with more fantasy than the Arabian Nights.

Tell the readers to yelp loud and long if they like my Western fantasy—and to keep kinda quiet ifn they don't.

The Old Word Wrangler,

L. Ron Hubbard.

If they like it, Mr. Hubbard, we'll send you to yore cupboard to dish us up some more.

From the June 1, 1940, issue of *Wild West Weekly.*

THE GOLDEN AGE OF SCIENCE FICTION

CHANGING A GENRE

By the end of 1937, L. Ron Hubbard had proven he could glide with protean ease from genre to genre—adventure, western, mystery, detective, romance—and was regularly featured in such acknowledged "crown jewels" of the pulp fiction world as *Adventure* and *Argosy*. Not bad for a young writer whose first commercially published fiction had appeared only three years before. But that wasn't all.

As mentioned, his first hardcover novel, the historical adventure *Buckskin Brigades,* had been received in August 1937 with

The fifteen-episode Columbia Pictures 1937 box-office-hit super serial *The Secret of Treasure Island*, adapted for the screen by L. Ron Hubbard from his novel **Murder at Pirate Castle**.

critical and commercial acclaim, including that of the *New York Times,* which applauded its "freshness and sparkle, decidedly rare in this type of romance." Propelled by his capacity for high-speed, quality output (some one hundred novels and stories published in less than three years), and his enthusiastically dedicated following in tow, Hubbard went to Hollywood at the invitation of Columbia Pictures. There, he adapted his novel *Murder at Pirate Castle*—originally intended for *Argosy*—for the screen as *The Secret of Treasure Island.* It became a centerpiece of the studio's scheduled big-budget super serials, a weekly staple for millions of moviegoers. Meanwhile, even as he generated a steady flow of magazine fiction for his editors in New York, Hubbard collaborated with Norvell Page—creator of the pulp fiction hero "The Spider"—on Warner Bros.' *The Spider Returns* and on Columbia's *The Adventures of the Mysterious Pilot* and *The Great Adventures of Wild Bill Hickok.*

By the spring of 1938, with his now well-established stature as a writer—or, in the words of author and critic Robert Silverberg, as a "master of the art of narrative"—Hubbard was invited to apply his gifts for succinct characterization, original plot, deft pacing and imaginative action to a genre that was new, and essentially foreign, to him—science fiction and fantasy. The reverberations of that invitation continue to this day, representing the seminal transformation of a genre through heightened imagination and broader literary dimension, and, ultimately, the evolution of speculative fiction into its modern form.

How this transformation came about is nowhere better described than by Hubbard himself in the introduction to his culminating science fiction epic, *Battlefield Earth:*

"It will probably be best to return to the day in 1938 when I first entered this field, the day I met John W. Campbell, Jr., a day in the very dawn of what has come to be known as The Golden Age of science fiction. I was quite ignorant of the field and regarded it, in fact, a bit diffidently. . . . I had been summoned to the vast old building on Seventh Avenue in dusty, dirty, old New York by the very top brass of Street and Smith publishing company. . . .

"In those days," Hubbard continues, "when the top brass of a publishing company—particularly one as old [1885] and prestigious as Street and Smith—'invited' a writer to visit, it was like being commanded to appear before the king or receiving a court summons. You arrived, you sat there obediently, and you spoke when you were spoken to."

L. Ron Hubbard, New York City, circa 1938: Well over one hundred of his novels and stories had already been published in a range of genres, and the first of his seminal works of speculative fiction was to appear that year.

Posters for **The Phantom Duel** and **Buried Alive**, from *The Secret of Treasure Island* series.

What the Street & Smith executives wanted became quickly apparent. One of their magazines was adrift in perilously competitive waters with its stories about "machines and machinery." The publishing giant had tried everything, even serial name changes from *Astounding Stories of Super-Science* to *Astounding Stories,* and finally, with the March 1938 issue, to the name by which it would come to dominate the field, *Astounding Science Fiction.* The pall of the Depression still hovered grayly over the country and the competition for reader loyalties from other magazines, including those in Street & Smith's own vast stable, was fierce. The usual cover price of twenty cents—and I remember my mother making this point to me, emphatically and often—represented a considerable outlay from an average family's resources.

Street & Smith's top brass, Hubbard tells us, knew that in this kind of competitive climate "you had to have *people* in stories." They knew with certainty, as well, that Hubbard could write powerfully and discerningly about people. They knew it from his work generally, and they knew it, with special familiarity, from the fiction he had produced for Street & Smith's own magazines, *Top-Notch,* *Western Story* and *Wild West Weekly.*

While continuing to produce a steady stream of magazine fiction for his editors in New York, Hubbard worked on the screenplays for such other Columbia releases as *The Adventures of the Mysterious Pilot* and *The Great Adventures of Wild Bill Hickok.*

Hubbard wasn't immediately receptive to the idea. He didn't write about ray guns, machines or robots, he told the executives (although many years later he did write a story about robots and mistaken identities—"Battling Bolto"—for another magazine). He wrote about people, he demurred. But Street & Smith's leadership insisted: that was exactly why they were turning to him.

Hubbard, still hesitant, agreed—reflecting, as he recollected later, that being a successful writer in other genres "was hardly reason to say no to the biggest publisher of the day."

At that point in the meeting, Hubbard recalls, the executives called in John W. Campbell, Jr., the twenty-eight-year-old writer-turned-fledgling-editor only recently hired to run *Astounding Science Fiction*. It would prove a historic, though not altogether felicitous, first encounter of powerful personalities.

As a writer, Campbell had given strong, early indications of his creative viewpoint with a five-part series called "The Mighty Machine." Hubbard recalls that Campbell—the man "who dominated the whole field of sf as its virtual czar until his death in 1971"—had definite ideas about science fiction that did not, then, appear to include publishing the work of a writer whose reputation, however formidable, had been achieved with tales of adventure, the old West and the strategies of detection.

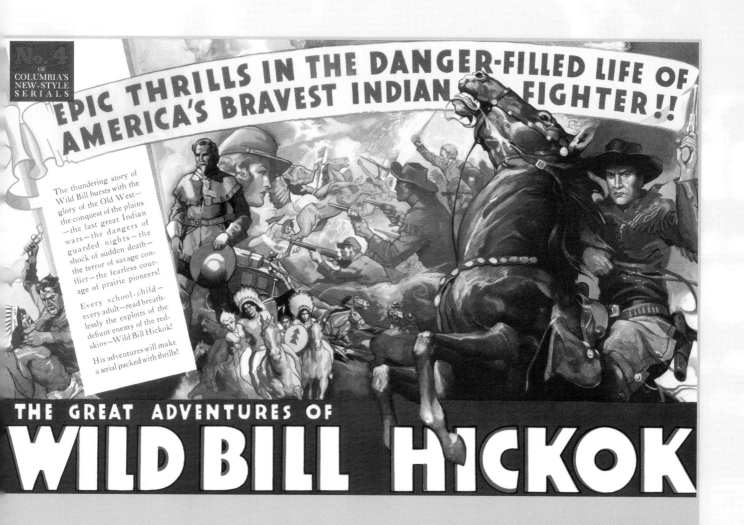

Campbell argued and resisted, but the Street & Smith executives were firm. He was, they told him, "going to get *people* into his stories and get something going besides *machines*." Campbell, at last, relented, and out of that somewhat contentious beginning, Ron Hubbard and John Campbell began a working relationship—and a friendship—with profound ramifications and enduring significance for the world of speculative fiction.

"The Dangerous Dimension," L. Ron Hubbard's first science fiction story (he later said he considered it fantasy, but critical opinion has consistently embraced it as innovative science fiction), was published in the July 1938 issue of *Astounding Science Fiction*. It was the first of thirty-one novels and stories—under Hubbard's name and such pen names as Rene Lafayette and Kurt von Rachen—that would appear in that magazine alone over the next twelve years and prove instrumental in making *Astounding* the undisputed epitome of popular science fiction.

With "The Dangerous Dimension," the genre took a sharp, humanizing turn that would permanently transform it in ways that probably few who read the story at the time could envision. One reader, however—a young fan named Isaac Asimov—wrote a letter to Campbell asking, simply, for "some more from L. Ron Hubbard, please."

There are, of course, no ray guns, robots or machine societies in "The Dangerous Dimension." Instead, the "dimension" is the most dangerous of all—the mind of untidy, diffident Yamouth University philosopher Dr. Henry Mudge, who undergoes a startling personality change when he stumbles upon a mathematical door to a "negative dimension" that enables him instantly to go anywhere he thinks of—Paris, the Central Park Zoo, the Moon, Mars—even when he doesn't want to go.

In just a few thousand words, Hubbard had given science fiction an actual "person"—a fully realized, if initially unprepossessing, character "hero"—and entry into an imagined world extrapolated from the small, prosaic details of the real one. As always for Hubbard, detail dominated: the paperwork clutter of Dr. Mudge's office; his frayed carpet slippers and the glasses perched precariously on his nose; the single tuft of fur on an orangutan in the zoo; the saucers on a Parisian restaurant table. They are all tangible and immediate. Yet they are also the materials of the negative dimension Hubbard describes, in a capsule parody of the long, tedious sermons on science that cluttered so much of earlier science fiction, as "no dimension. The existence of nothing as something—"

Hubbard had, of course, fashioned an earlier story of the speculative, out-of-the-ordinary event in a commonplace setting—the impossible that could possibly happen to anyone—in his 1936 "The Death Flyer." Revisiting the impossible as

John W. Campbell, Jr. (above right), editor of *Astounding* and *Unknown,* with L. Ron Hubbard.

reality in "The Dangerous Dimension," Hubbard promptly explored it even more extensively and with compelling effect. In his second story for *Astounding,* "The Tramp" (September through November 1938), he gave the concept an ominous twist. "The Tramp" tells of a hobo, suddenly endowed with phenomenal mental powers after experimental brain surgery saves his life, who attempts to seize control of the United States government.

"The Tramp," which echoes conceptually through many other Hubbard stories to follow, meshes the speculative and the prosaic by juxtaposing a hobo, a common enough feature of American life in those days, and the bizarre and dangerous tele-kinetic powers he acquires. Hubbard would return again and again to this technique of blending the familiar and the arcane in greater and lesser ways—in the parallel worlds of *Slaves of Sleep,* the virtual realities of *Typewriter in the Sky,* the macabre shadows of *Fear,* the mundane details of a taxi and a lone man leaning on a walking stick in the alternate future of *The End Is Not Yet,* the farmer and his horse at an invisible intersection in time in "The Crossroads," and the sun-dappled meadow that the space-voyaging physician sees through his window in "Ole Doc Methuselah."

Shortly after L. Ron Hubbard began redefining science fiction, he was joined in the pages of *Astounding Science Fiction* by the first-published stories of such emerging contemporaries as A.E. van Vogt, Theodore Sturgeon and the legendary Robert Heinlein.

Recall that even at the beginning, with "The Dangerous Dimension," Hubbard regarded what he was writing as fantasy, not science fiction. In his *Battlefield Earth* introduction, L. Ron Hubbard describes fantasy as "any fiction that takes up elements such as spiritualism, mythology, magic, divination, the supernatural, and so on." Science fiction, he postulates, "is the herald of possibility." Fantasy, on the other hand, "gives you no limits at all."

Blinded by the brilliant sheen of the floor—numbed by the bombarding thought-waves of the Martians, Mudge stumbled and fell to his knees.

"The Dangerous Dimension," as it appeared in the July 1938 issue of *Astounding Science Fiction*.

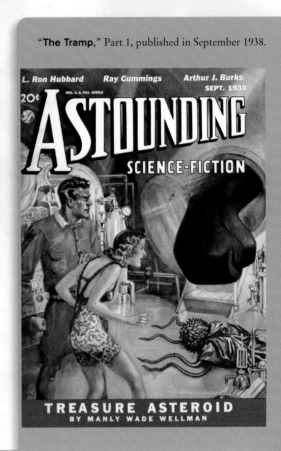

"The Tramp," Part 1, published in September 1938.

L. Ron Hubbard   Ray Cummings   Arthur J. Burks

20¢   SEPT. 1938

ASTOUNDING
SCIENCE-FICTION

TREASURE ASTEROID
BY MANLY WADE WELLMAN

L. RON HUBBARD

tells of a weak little man that Fate cursed with an accident—that gave him a mighty power! His friendly glance cured any ill—his angry gaze was Death. By accident a doctor had given him the legendary Evil Eye!

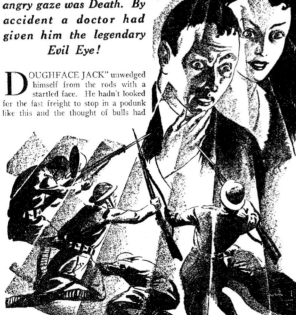

THE TRAMP

The first part of a great three-part serial.

"DOUGHFACE JACK" unwedged himself from the rods with a startled face. He hadn't looked for the fast freight to stop in a podunk like this and the thought of bulls had no more than flashed through his mind than he saw some legs coming and stopping at intervals along the cars. From the stick he knew it was an irate brakie, already twice dodged en route.

Anxiously, Doughface sought to scramble out from under and so make the other side of the train. But the engineer backed a few feet with a jolt and, not knowing when it would happen again, Doughface took his chance.

He rocketed like a rabbit to the cinders and got one awe-inspiring glimpse of the six-foot brakie. He started to run, but in the other direction came somebody with a sheriff's paunch.

There was only one thing for it. The hounds had sighted the hare and Doughface couldn't trust his short legs on the level. He grabbed the handholds and started up the car.

"Come back here!" bellowed the brakie.

"Stop!" roared the sheriff.

Doughface scrambled for altitude as heavy boots ground cinders just under him. He was panting as he made the top of the car. He glanced back to see that the brakie was coming up the same way and the sheriff had taken the other ladder. The sheriff had a gun in his hand.

Doughface took a sweeping look at the town he had uncovered. An old gent waited at the crossing in a Model T Ford. A sign said "Centerville—Population 2,000." It was better than nothing. Doughface leaped for the other

It soon became evident to John Campbell that of the many stories he was receiving, particularly from Hubbard, a substantial number belonged more clearly in the category of fantasy than science fiction. He quickly convinced Street & Smith to launch a new magazine to accommodate the fantasy stories he was getting from Hubbard. It was called *Unknown* (later *Unknown Worlds*) and Campbell was its first editor. In its comparatively brief life span—March 1939 to October 1943, when wartime paper shortages prematurely dictated its demise—*Unknown* indisputably became the foremost fantasy publication of its time, and its tapestried tales of mythic worlds, inward dimensions and strange journeys to the edge of the light became the paradigm for much of contemporary fantasy.

L. Ron Hubbard's innovative stories and novels contributed instrumentally to *Unknown*'s rapid rise and influence. It was, in fact, the first issue of the magazine, in March 1939, that heralded the publication in the next month's issue of Hubbard's initial story for *Unknown,* "The Ultimate Adventure." Campbell hailed the upcoming tale of a penniless young man's perilous journey into a jeweled Arabian Nights mirror world as "a thirty-thousand-word definition of *Unknown*'s pure entertainment!"

It was that, indeed.

Even before *Unknown*'s debut, Campbell had learned of Hubbard's intimate familiarity with the traditions of fantasy and lore displayed years earlier in works such as Washington Irving's *Tales of the Alhambra* and Sir Richard Burton's translation of the tales of the Arabian Nights. That knowledge convinced Campbell that stories in that tradition to appear in the pages of *Unknown* would be exclusively Hubbard's.

"**The Tramp,**" Part 2, published in October 1938. Pulp cover art by Howard V. Brown.

He was not recognized, and for a moment was at peace. Then— "It's him—him—the man with the Evil Eye!"

Synopsis:

DOUGHFACE JACK TURNS COP KILLER

Two Dead and Three Dying Following Tramps Arrest in Central Park

STILL LOOSE IN CITY!

THE TRAMP
by L. Ron Hubbard

A frightened little man possessed of a deadly power drives all New York—the Nation!—into panic fear!

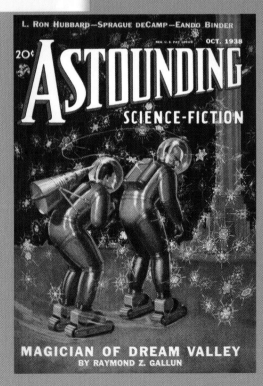

L. RON HUBBARD—SPRAGUE deCAMP—EANDO BINDER

OCT. 1938

20¢

ASTOUNDING
SCIENCE-FICTION

MAGICIAN OF DREAM VALLEY
BY RAYMOND Z. GALLUN

THE TRAMP

by L. Ron Hubbard

The bitter hate of a blind beggar hag—incarnated in a rejuvenated woman, drives a beaten, mild little tramp to autocratic rule through a terrible power—The Evil Eye.

PART III

Conclusion

Doughface Jack faltered. For the first time, he glared at a man who did not fall.

Harl Vincent — L. Ron Hubbard — Nat Schachner

20¢ **ASTOUNDING**
SCIENCE-FICTION

NOV. 1938

JUPITER, SEEN FROM GANYMEDE

REUNION ON GANYMEDE *by Clifford D. Simak*

Part 3 and the conclusion to **"The Tramp,"** published in November 1938. Pulp cover art by Howard V. Brown.

"I'm damn glad you'll be with us on the Arabian Nights stuff—" Campbell wrote, "and you needn't worry about having it yours. I've been telling a few of the boys to read Washington Irving as an example of pure fantasy and complete acceptance of magic, enchantment, et cetera, and adding that they aren't to do Arabian Nights because the field is preempted by you. It's been held open for you." Then, as if to preclude any misunderstanding, Campbell added, with final emphasis, "I'm reserving the Arabian Nights to you entirely."

Now, with "The Ultimate Adventure" already attracting wide attention (one reader called it simply "the best fantasy I have read in years"), and after a brief, but fascinating, foray into South Seas demonology in "Danger in the Dark," Hubbard produced a landmark work of the modern Arabian Nights style, the fantasy novel *Slaves of Sleep,* in the July 1939 issue of *Unknown.* The setting, though, was not ancient Baghdad but present-day Puget Sound in the Pacific Northwest. The protagonist, Jan Palmer, was no street urchin, but—at least initially—the somewhat unassertive heir to a shipping fortune. And there is, of course, a girl, Alice Hall, who leaves Jan breathless.

But then, with Hubbard's unmistakable touch, the lines between the real and the illusory, the here and now and the there and some other time, begin to blur and merge. There is an open antique copper jar, a dead professor, an angry jinni, the curse of Eternal Wakefulness and Palmer in jail, accused of murder.

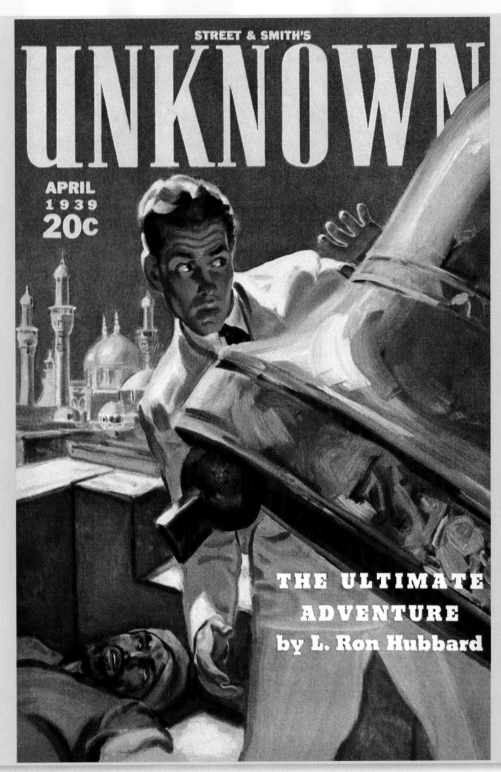

By L. Ron Hubbard

Slaves of Sleep, first published in July 1939. Cover art by H. Winfield Scott and interior illustrations by Edd Cartier.

Slaves of Sleep paperback edition, published in 1967. Cover art by Frank Kelly Freas.

And then, with lightning suddenness, Jan is Tiger, a buccaneer and a rogue. A girl named Wanna, who looks suspiciously like Alice, joins him in an arabesque realm of magic, sorcery and the all-powerful jinn—a world parallel to this one. Or do they actually intersect? No matter. It is a world both wonderful and dangerous, just like ours.

The impact of the novel was immediate. Author and editor Frederik Pohl remembers that *Slaves of Sleep* "became sort of a buzz word"—and, assuredly, it did. Asimov, again, wrote to Campbell, saying, "The yarn was a corker"—and it was. A letter "transmitted by Ray Bradbury" from the Los Angeles Science and Fantasy League applauded *Slaves of Sleep* and *The Ghoul*, Hubbard's next story in *Unknown*, as "the finest yet printed." And there was the reader from Durham, North Carolina, who protested that he didn't usually read pulp fiction but in this case he found *Slaves of Sleep* "stupendous, magnificent and entirely different . . . How about a sequel?"

Hardcover edition, published in 1948. Cover art by Hannes Bok.

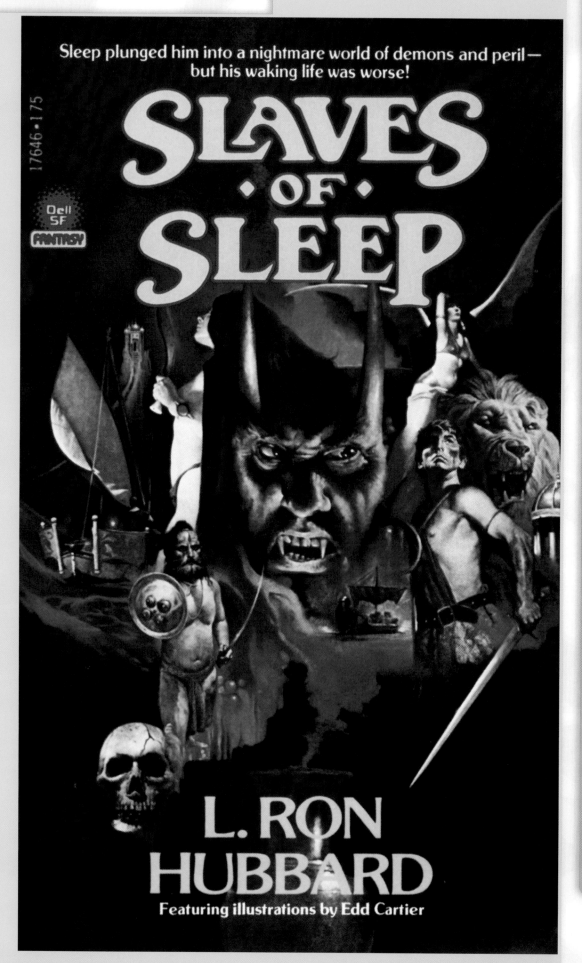

Sleep plunged him into a nightmare world of demons and peril—
but his waking life was worse!

SLAVES ·OF· SLEEP

Dell SF FANTASY

17646 • 175

L. RON HUBBARD

Featuring illustrations by Edd Cartier

Chinese translation of *Slaves of Sleep* (top), published in 1997. Italian edition (middle), published in 1998. Taiwanese edition (bottom), published in 2000.

There would be a sequel, of course—a celebrated one—but ten years, a world war and the tumultuous dawn of the Atomic Age would intervene before it appeared as *The Masters of Sleep* in the October 1950 issue of *Fantastic Adventures*. Announcing the "long-awaited sequel to his *Slaves of Sleep*" a month earlier, the magazine noted, without having to elaborate, that "an L. Ron Hubbard novel is always big news." It was also immediately clear that the story had lost none of its prismatic charm and that the author had lost none of his storytelling legerdemain. Opening with a thundering naval engagement between warring factions of the jinn fleet, the story swiftly introduces us to a somewhat older Jan/Tiger and Alice/Wanna, who, essentially, rediscover adventure and each other. Once more, a reader's letter said it most cogently: "*Masters of Sleep* was the best story I have read in a long time."

When *Slaves of Sleep* was first published, John W. Campbell, Jr., sent Hubbard a letter that shines a revealing light on the crucial role the author was playing in the fortunes of both *Unknown* and *Astounding Science Fiction*. Noting at the outset that he had mailed Hubbard the largest check in *Unknown*'s history, and the second largest in the combined history of *Unknown* and *Astounding*, Campbell went on to enjoin Hubbard to "please start now on your next Arabian Nights yarn. What'll it be about? I'd like to get it in about four weeks. . . .

The sequel to *Slaves of Sleep*, entitled **The Masters of Sleep**, released in October 1950 in *Fantastic Adventures*. Cover art by Robert Gibson Jones.

"*I remember reading* **Slaves of Sleep** *and enjoying it and fantasizing about it. That was one of the reasons you read that sort of story, to sort of lose yourself in that world and feel what it would be like if you could be there.*

"**Slaves of Sleep** *became sort of a buzz word.*

"*There are bits and pieces from Ron's work that became part of the language in ways that very few other writers managed. Even Heinlein did not have quite that sort of effect.*"

—Frederik Pohl

Illustrations by Edd Cartier
for *The Ghoul*.

"I'm having a hell of a time," Campbell added, "getting the long stuff, because I consistently and firmly bounce anything below grade B+, and all the novels seem to run about grade C+." And then he reminded his star writer, "Just because *Unknown*'s going, don't forget *Astounding* still uses 85,000 words a month."

As it turned out, the letter was a striking portent of things to come, and a measure of how quickly—and how decisively—L. Ron Hubbard had moved to center stage in the world of speculative fiction.

Author and critic Damon Knight said it as definitively as anyone ever has when he wrote that L. Ron Hubbard "cut a swath across the science-fantasy world, the like of which has never been seen again."

There were, however, many facets to this picture. Perhaps two will help to illumine the whole.

In 1937, Catherine L. Moore, who went on to her own stellar career in science fiction, wrote with self-effacing candor to Hubbard: "Your taste is so much better than mine. . . . your very vivid and colorful descriptions come in small doses, instead of encrusting the story so thickly that one's slightly sick from the richness by the time the tale's finished.

"My stories," she continued, "are like making a meal off chocolate pie and plum pudding, while yours have a sufficient admixture of rare beef-steak and beer and salad to make the dessert welcome instead of cloying."

And there was Robert Heinlein, who said he had thought for years there were only two main plots for the human-interest story: boy-meets-girl and "The Little Tailor." But he credited L. Ron Hubbard with showing him a third: the man-who-learned-better.

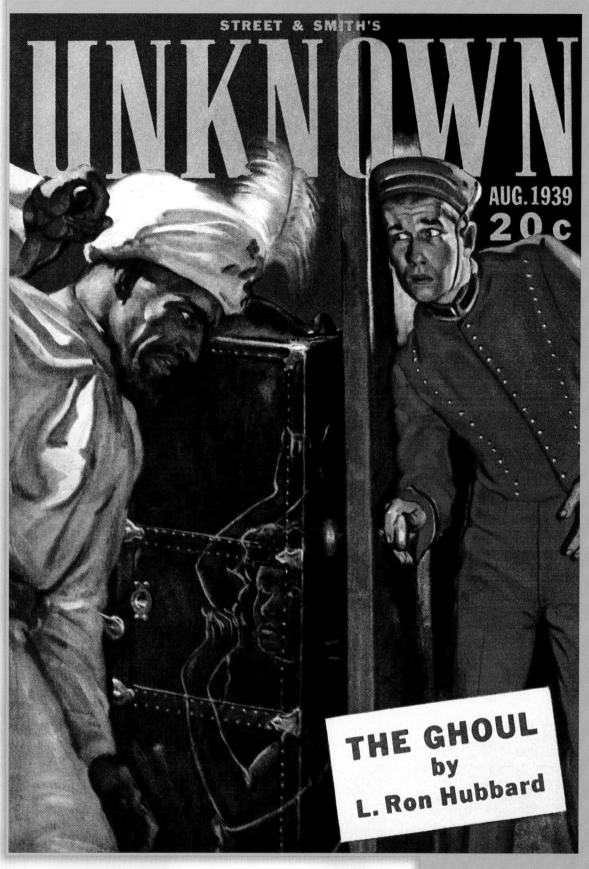

STREET & SMITH'S

UNKNOWN

AUG. 1939
20 c

THE GHOUL
by
L. Ron Hubbard

The Ghoul, published in August 1939. Cover art by Graves Gladney.

At this point, then, the scene was set for one of the most phenomenal periods in L. Ron Hubbard's career and arguably in the career of any writer. It came in 1940, when the strands of his astonishing productivity—particularly in science fiction and fantasy—came together in an immense outpouring of creativity and imagination.

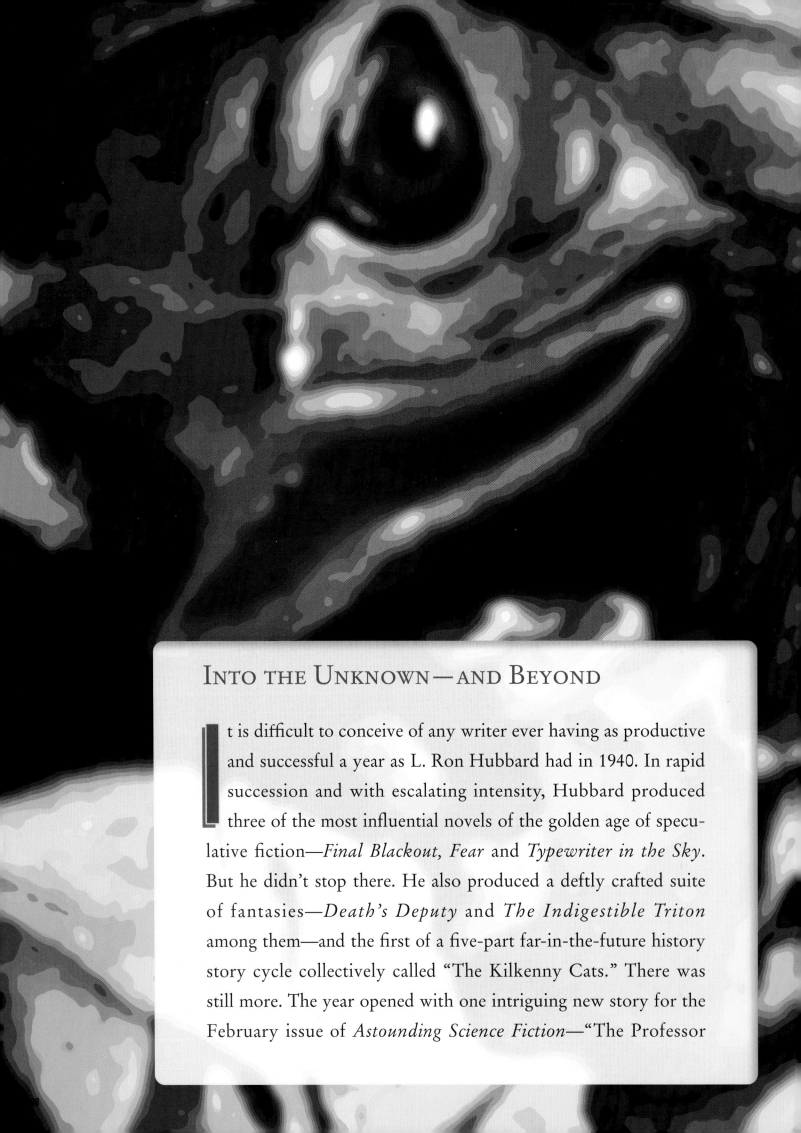

INTO THE UNKNOWN—AND BEYOND

It is difficult to conceive of any writer ever having as productive and successful a year as L. Ron Hubbard had in 1940. In rapid succession and with escalating intensity, Hubbard produced three of the most influential novels of the golden age of speculative fiction—*Final Blackout, Fear* and *Typewriter in the Sky*. But he didn't stop there. He also produced a deftly crafted suite of fantasies—*Death's Deputy* and *The Indigestible Triton* among them—and the first of a five-part far-in-the-future history story cycle collectively called "The Kilkenny Cats." There was still more. The year opened with one intriguing new story for the February issue of *Astounding Science Fiction*—"The Professor

Was a Thief," a wryly funny and inventive variation on the theme he had initially explored in "The Dangerous Dimension" and "The Tramp." But this time, when the Empire State Building, Grant's Tomb and Pennsylvania Station suddenly disappear, it's not the work of human telekinesis, but rather a cigarette lighter that has been reconfigured by a playful professor into an atomic accelerator that can miniaturize objects of assorted size and complexity and transport them to his model railroad. When the story was later anthologized in the 1949 *My Best Science Fiction Story,* Hubbard explained that "it changed a trend. In the days when it was first published all the professors of science fiction were blowing up worlds, creating new universes. . . . My professor had another idea."

It was an idea with such durable appeal that a radio adaptation of it aired on NBC in 1950 as an episode in the network's highly popular *Dimension X* series. It was also a motif that Hubbard, writing as Rene Lafayette, would re-examine with

Ron returning to Seattle under Explorers Club flag number 105, aboard the *Magician,* in December 1940—the same year **Final Blackout**, **Fear** and **Typewriter in the Sky** were published.

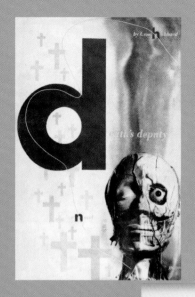
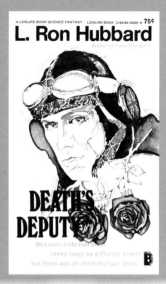

Hardcover edition of *Death's Deputy*, left, published in 1948. Paperback edition, center, published in 1970. Japanese translation, right, published in 1992.

a more ominous edge in "One Was Stubborn," in the November 1940 edition of *Astounding*, when an elderly gentleman discovers that things vanish when he stops thinking about them. Indeed, it was a theme Hubbard would revisit in other stories, in other years, with imaginative variations. "The Room" is one example, with its inventory of strange souvenirs with even stranger transforming properties. Another is "The Obsolete Weapon," in which a pen-like device resurrects the gladiatorial perils of imperial Rome.

February 1940 also saw *Unknown*'s publication of L. Ron Hubbard's merger of action-adventure and speculative fiction in the novel called *Death's Deputy*. An artful weaving of the fierce thrills of action stories with the mysteriously haunted life of a fighter pilot named Clayton McLean who brings disaster to those around him while he himself is inexplicably spared, the novel was a sensational hit, which came as no surprise to John Campbell. He had tantalized *Unknown*'s readers the month before the novel's debut with the question, "You may miss *Death's Deputy* coming next month—but will HE MISS YOU?" It was, of course, an irresistible invitation. And the story—with its fury of blazing aerial combat and its sense of the unknowable folding darkly around McLean and his wife—delivered a powerful emotional punch. Hubbard's theme—"servants of disaster" who enjoy a strangely charmed life—had come out of a meeting with Campbell the previous September. Hubbard later described the conversation this way:

"He and I thrashed around until we got the idea of a man who officiates, all unwillingly, for the god of destruction. Without volition on his part he causes accidents." Thoroughly researching the concept, including examining insurance company statistics just as he had for his fabled "Hell Job" series in *Argosy*, Hubbard concluded that "There are people, then, who seem to be magnets for destruction. Although rarely touched themselves, things happen all around them."

Hence, the ill-starred Clayton McLean—"Death's Deputy"—in a story later described by a reviewer as "L. Ron Hubbard at his very best, and what reader could ask for more?" There was, however, one other aspect of the appearance of *Death's Deputy* in *Unknown* that enhanced its already considerable impact—the cover painting by master illustrator Edd Cartier. With its glaring devil centerpiece and its brilliant orange and red colors, it was, by any measure, the most celebrated cover art in *Unknown*'s history, and close to its last. Shortly afterward, the magazine went to a prim all-print cover format.

L. Ron Hubbard had once told an interviewer that after he had written a story it existed as an individual piece of work and he then couldn't remember a time when it was not written. It was that sense of the story's existence as a vital creative entity that Cartier, in particular, could capture and express visually.

Death's Deputy was the cover story in the February 1940 issue of *Unknown*. Cover art and illustration by Edd Cartier.

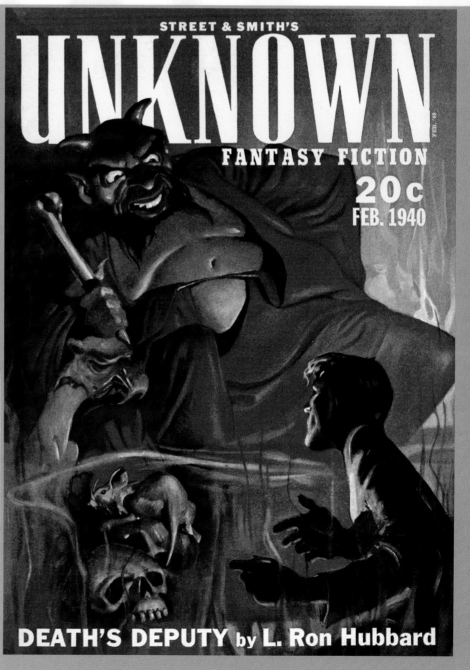

ASTOUNDING

SCIENCE-FICTION
A STREET & SMITH PUBLICATION

20¢
APR. 1940

FINAL BLACKOUT" by L. Ron Hubbard

"One of the most eagerly awaited returns from the war was that of L. Ron Hubbard. Hubbard's science fiction reputation had been made and nailed down for all time with his incomparable classic, **Final Blackout***, but his overall reputation was based on such novels for* Unknown *as* **Fear, Death's Deputy, Slaves of Sleep, The Case of the Friendly Corpse, The Ghoul,** *and others."*

—Alva Rogers, *A Requiem for* Astounding

Final Blackout, published in three parts in *Astounding Science Fiction* in April, May and June 1940. Cover art by Hubert Rogers.

Cartier, who had illustrated *Slaves of Sleep,* would apply his distinctive artistry to *Fear* later in 1940 in *Unknown;* to *The Case of the Friendly Corpse* when that story introduced its lively retinue of wizards, posthumous sultans and magic potions in the pages of the same magazine in August 1941; to the timeless exploits of "Ole Doc Methuselah" in *Astounding* in the closing years of the decade; and to the fantastic world of *The Indigestible Triton.*

Dear Mr. Campbell:

Reader's report on Astounding for 1940:

Ten best stories:
1. "Final Blackout," by L. Ron Hubbard. It's a classic. Nothing of the same type will ever surpass it.

From the April 1941 issue of *Astounding Science Fiction.*

The publication of Hubbard's *Triton* as the cover story in the April 1940 issue of *Unknown* and the simultaneous appearance of his *Final Blackout* on the cover of *Astounding Science Fiction* that same month was an uncommon achievement in the publishing history of science fiction and fantasy. But it was not really a surprise. On the one hand, it was a dramatic affirmation of Hubbard's remarkable range and versatility. On the other, the stories themselves simply compelled recognition.

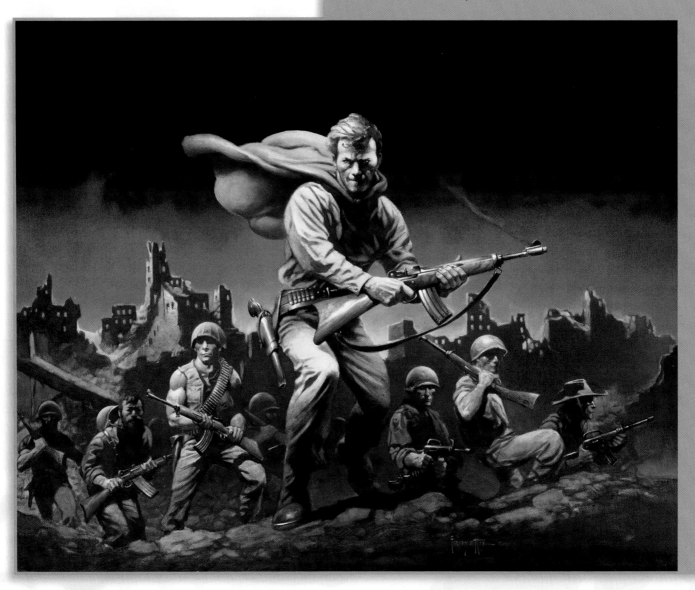

The Lieutenant, artwork by Frank Frazetta based on the book *Final Blackout*.

Final Blackout has been translated into six languages: Chinese, Estonian, French, Italian, Korean and Lithuanian. Shown below (left to right) are the French trade paperback, 1992; French paperback, 1995; Korean, 1995; Italian, 1996.

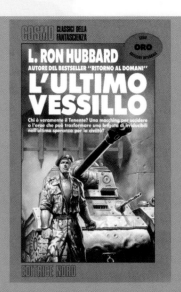

The Indigestible Triton was sheer, ebullient entertainment, with a hero, fleeing from an interfering family to the refuge of a fishing trip, who finds himself with a problem far more formidable than obnoxious relatives—an ill-humored demigod of the sea.

A charming literary divertissement—then and now—the story struck a responsive chord with both readers and the critical community. The *New York Herald Tribune* later characterized it as "a free fantasia on mermen and other unlikely sea denizens which reaches delightful heights." A reader, at the time, approvingly ranked it "well at the top . . . of all the hilarious stories I have read." And Frederik Pohl, writing in *Super Science Stories,* concluded that it was "fast and funny and altogether entertaining."

Meanwhile, L. Ron Hubbard was moving across another creative threshold with a novel of genuinely staggering power and significance—*Final Blackout.* Published as the Second World War raged across the face of Europe with its shadows lengthening everywhere, *Final Blackout* unfolded in the April, May and June issues of *Astounding* with the literary and emotional impact of a lightning bolt.

Universally regarded as one of the greatest novels of science fiction's golden age and among the most influential works of twentieth-century military science fiction, *Final Blackout* envisioned an apocalyptic war that would go on and on into a future tormented by endless combat and cynical political opportunism, with Europe—and the world—indelibly scarred by weapons of biological and atomic fury.

It was an astonishing vision of what could happen and a chilling warning, which has echoed across more than six decades, of what may still happen. It is also, in the estimation of Robert Heinlein, "as perfect a piece of science fiction as has ever been written."

In *Final Blackout* Hubbard also gave us a larger-than-life, combat-wise, principled protagonist. Known only as "the Lieutenant," his deep moral concern for his brigade of irregulars—"The Unkillables" (Hubbard's work-in-progress title for *Final Blackout*)—became the measure of the quintessential leader. In the end, it is up to this band of survivors, led by a man whose very anonymity symbolizes a transcending clarity of purpose and the conviction that the individual can make a difference, to salvage what they can of their lives and their civilization.

Later, in 1948, after Hubbard had returned from four years of active duty in World War II as a U.S. naval officer in the Pacific theater, he wrote a preface and a new dedication to a hardcover edition of *Final Blackout*—"To the men and officers with whom I served in World War II, first phase, 1941–1945"—that excited new discussion and endless interpretations of the novel's complex meaning and portent.

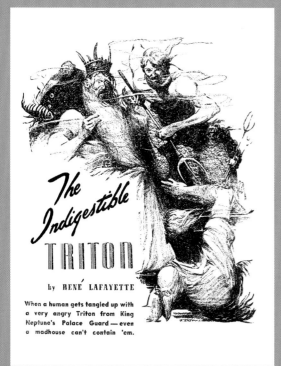

The Indigestible Triton, published under the pen name Rene Lafayette in April 1940. Cover art by Edd Cartier.

Final Blackout has remained in print, in one edition after another, and in a growing number of languages—French, Italian, Chinese, Korean and Lithuanian among them—for more than sixty years. A superb blending of Hubbard's high-paced action, knowledgeable detail and defining characterization with a theme of visionary insight, *Final Blackout* and the Lieutenant remain icons of the golden age's literary legacy.

Over the years, *Final Blackout* has been variously acclaimed as the archetypal "survivalist" story, the exemplar of "future war" novels, and as a trendsetting "alternate history." Arguably, it is all of these. But *Final Blackout* is also best defined by its readers and fans. One letter published in *Astounding* said simply, "It's a classic. Nothing of the same type will ever surpass it." Another applauded it as "the best science fiction story I have ever read . . . undoubtedly the best story of any type I have ever read." And still another wrote of being moved "perilously close to tears" by the novel's ending.

Final Blackout does, indeed, have a classic, lyric power, exemplified nowhere more expressively than in its final lines:

"Above the Byward Gate on Tower Hill that flag still flies; the gold is so faded that only one who knows can trace the marks which once made so clear the insignia of a lieutenant, the white field is bleached and patched where furious winds have torn it. It is the first thing men look to in the morning and the last thing men see when the sky fades out and the clear, sad notes of retreat are sounded by the British bugler on Tower Hill.

"That flag still flies, and on the plaque below are graven the words:

"*When that command remains, no matter what happens to its officer, he has not failed.*"

Ron, in the words of John W. Campbell, Jr., lived the richly versatile life of a true Renaissance man.

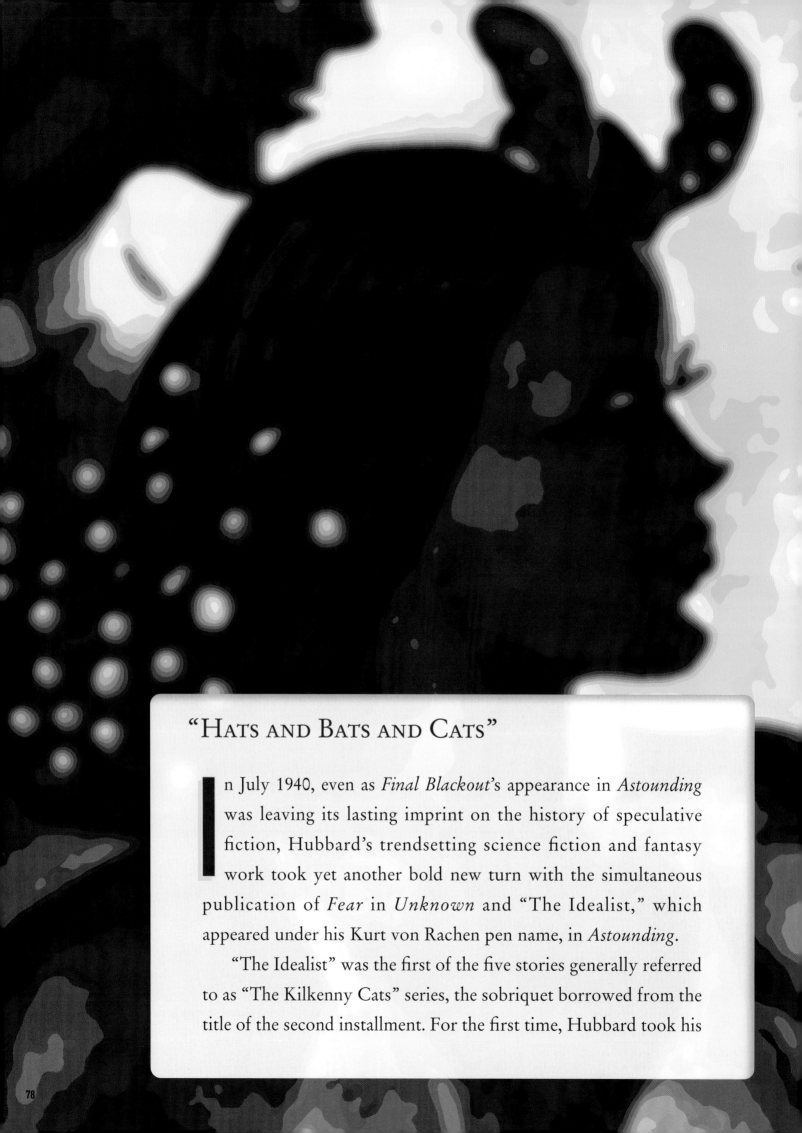

"HATS AND BATS AND CATS"

I n July 1940, even as *Final Blackout*'s appearance in *Astounding* was leaving its lasting imprint on the history of speculative fiction, Hubbard's trendsetting science fiction and fantasy work took yet another bold new turn with the simultaneous publication of *Fear* in *Unknown* and "The Idealist," which appeared under his Kurt von Rachen pen name, in *Astounding*.

"The Idealist" was the first of the five stories generally referred to as "The Kilkenny Cats" series, the sobriquet borrowed from the title of the second installment. For the first time, Hubbard took his readers into deep space, and did so with his signature color, action and sharply focused characterization. Set in the year 2893, the resourceful "idealist" Steve Gailbraith and his rebellious colleague, Vicki Stalton, are pitted against the despotic Fagar, the Deliverer, in a story permeated with intrigue and the infinite peril of travel to new worlds. The five stories appeared over a period of a year and a half, culminating with "The Rebel" in February 1942, and enjoyed enormous reader support. One enthusiast, for example, informed John Campbell the story "was so good it hurt to read it. I'll never get over that yarn."

In retrospect, of course, the "Cats," as we aficionados knew them, were a foreshadowing of larger worlds to come—the "Ole Doc Methuselah" and "Conquest of Space" series in the late 1940s and Ron's epic 1980s curtain call, *Battlefield Earth* and the *Mission Earth* dekalogy.

"**The Idealist**," the first of five stories collectively called "The Kilkenny Cats," appeared in the July 1940 issue under the pen name Kurt von Rachen. Cover art by Hubert Rogers. Illustration by R. Isip.

THE IDEALIST

By Kurt von Rachen

Illustrated by R. Isip

Idealists generally make revolutions—and either die in them, or are condemned by the men they fought for!

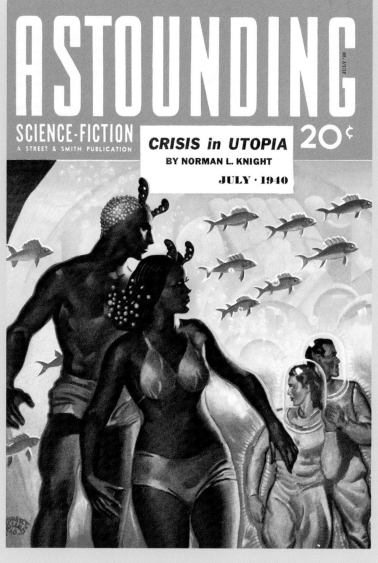

The second in "The Kilkenny Cats" series, entitled **"The Kilkenny Cats,"** appeared in the September 1940 issue of *Astounding Science Fiction.* Cover art by Hubert Rogers.

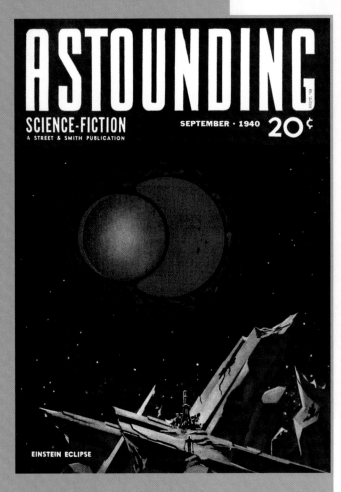

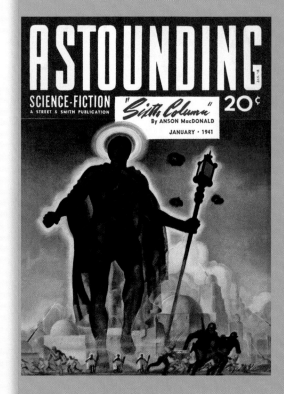

The third story in "The Kilkenny Cats" series, **"The Traitor,"** appeared in the January 1941 issue. Cover art by Hubert Rogers.

"You've given them all the food ñand weapons," Blacker howled. Fagar's representative smiled. "But you've got more men—and the water. Good-by."

THE MUTINEERS

By Kurt von Rachen

The Kilkenny Cats—even supplied with transport by Gailbraith's efforts—still wanted to destroy themselves!

Illustrated by Schneeman

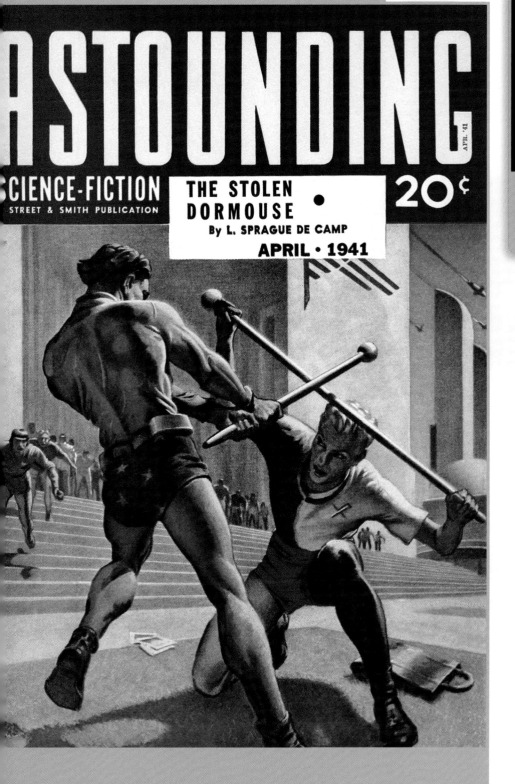

"**The Mutineers**," fourth in "The Kilkenny Cats" series, appeared in this April 1941 issue. Cover art by Hubert Rogers.

ASTOUNDING
SCIENCE-FICTION
STREET & SMITH PUBLICATION
20¢
APR. '41

THE STOLEN DORMOUSE
By L. SPRAGUE DE CAMP
APRIL · 1941

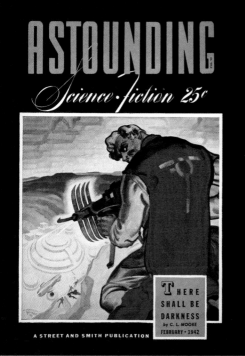

The fifth and last story in "The Kilkenny Cats" series, "**The Rebels**," was published in February 1942. Cover art by Hubert Rogers.

Fear, meanwhile, was instantly acknowledged as a classic. It broke new ground in horror and suspense fiction, and profoundly influenced the work of the field's masters, from Ray Bradbury to Stephen King.

Described by science fiction grandmaster Jack Williamson as "the triumphant pioneer of psychological thrillers," by author Robert Silverberg as "a classic masterpiece of psychological horror," and by author and critic Algis Budrys as simply "a big goddam lighthouse . . . one of the biggest milestones in the field," *Fear* forever changed the tone, mood, setting, narrative energy and direction of horror fiction.

Hubbard had offered glimpses of his new vision of horror in earlier stories—"The Death Flyer," "The Dangerous Dimension" and "The Tramp." Ordinary people, in an ordinary setting, experience something out of the ordinary, something that irrevocably changes them and the world around them. The magic is in the suggestion the author leaves behind that it could happen to anyone.

In *Fear*, the innocuously prosaic becomes an unremitting nightmare, introduced with a quiet sense of foreboding in the famous opening lines of the novel:

"Lurking, that lovely spring day, in the office of Dr. Chalmers, Atworthy College Medical Clinic, there might have been two small spirits of the air, pressed back into the dark shadow behind the door, avoiding as far as possible the warm sunlight which fell gently upon the rug."

The reader immediately knows that something is not quite right. But not what. And not why. Not yet.

The patient being examined is ethnology professor James Lowry, who has announced publicly that he doesn't believe in spirits, witches or demons. At least not until three o'clock in the afternoon of this otherwise normal spring day, in front of the quite ordinary house of an academic associate, when he suddenly loses his hat and four hours of his life. Abruptly, Lowry is plunged into a macabre world of night without day, of strange figures out of time, of "hats and bats and cats"—a litany Hubbard uses with mounting, spellbinding effect—and a secret evil that whispers to him from the darkness: "If you find your hat you'll find your four hours, and if you find your four hours then you will die!"

The climax, a classically pure and powerful "moment of truth," is abrupt and breathtaking—"a horrifying emotional punch," as one reviewer described it.

Hubbard began work on *Fear*—its working title was "Phantasmagoria"—in January 1940. His customary practice was to visualize a story completely and then to sit down and write it, straight through, with whirlwind speed. But by his own account, *Fear* came more slowly. "I finally got the plot of it licked," he wrote to a friend, describing his realized conception of a main character who unexpectedly loses hours from his life.

"He strives to locate his deeds while missing everywhere but in the right place, for he fears to look there," Hubbard explained. As for style—and *Fear* is a mesmerizing triumph of style—Hubbard added: "And I think a nice, delicate style is best suited. Paint everything in sweetness and light and then begin to dampen it, not with the style, but with the events themselves."

In the preceding issue of *Unknown*, John Campbell had warned his readers not to miss Hubbard's story. "*Fear*," he said, "has been built of nightmare stuff."

It was. It is. And its impact was immediate, genre shaping and permanent. Literary historian David Hartwell has applauded it as "one of the foundations of the contemporary horror genre, widely influential, and powerfully effective. . . . From Ray Bradbury to Stephen King, a literary debt is owed to L. Ron Hubbard for *Fear*."

Bradbury, indeed, has acknowledged that the novel "deeply influenced me when I was twenty years old" and was a "landmark novel in my life"—a sentiment underscored by author Ray Faraday Nelson, who has said that Hubbard's stories, but *Fear* in particular, "directly influenced all my work."

A reader called *Fear* "an epic . . . a classic of characterization." A reviewer said, "Hubbard defines the essence of what it means to be afraid." And author and critic James Blish brought still another literary perspective to it, assessing *Fear* as "an intellectual achievement of the first magnitude."

Not surprisingly, *Fear*'s publishing history has been extraordinary. It has been rereleased ten times by six different American publishers in paperback, hardback and audio editions, has been translated into nineteen languages—it's *Das Grauen (The Terror)* in German, *Dødens Timer (The Hour of Death)* in Danish, *Au Bout du Cauchemar (Descent Into Nightmare)* in French, *Le Quattro Ore del Terrore (The Four Hours of Terror)* in Italian—and remains a perennial bestseller, including a digital bestseller in eBook format, in various countries around the world.

Perhaps the last word, however, should come from that master of the modern horror story, Stephen King:

47 West Broadway, Bangor, Maine 04401

L. Ron Hubbard's Fear is one of the few books in the chiller genre which actually merits employment of the overworked adjective "classic," as in "This is a classic tale of creeping, surreal menace and horror." If you're not averse to a case of the cold chills--a rather bad one--and you've never read Fear, I urge you to do so. Don't even wait for a dark and stormy night. This is one of the really, really good ones.

Stephen King

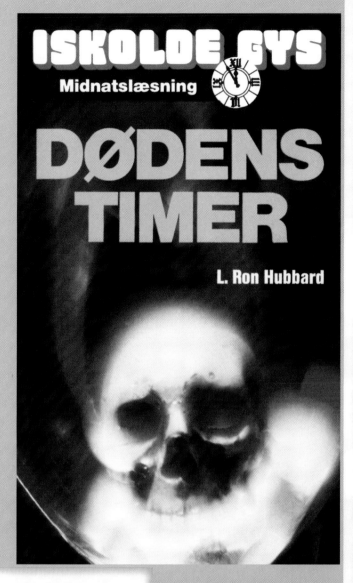

ISKOLDE GYS

Midnatslæsning

DØDENS TIMER

L. Ron Hubbard

Danish edition, published in 1968.

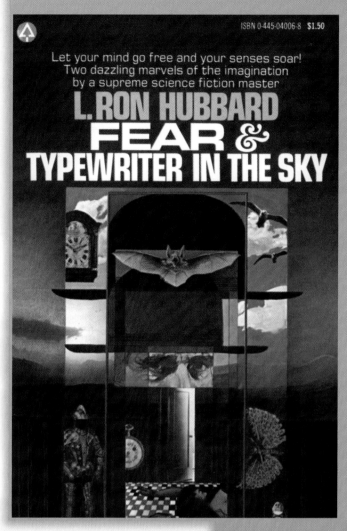

ISBN 0-445-04006-8 $1.50

Let your mind go free and your senses soar!
Two dazzling marvels of the imagination
by a supreme science fiction master

L. RON HUBBARD
FEAR &
TYPEWRITER IN THE SKY

Fear has been translated into nine-teen languages since its original 1940 publication in *Unknown*.

English paperback edition, published in 1977 with *Typewriter in the Sky*.

Japanese hardcover edition, left, published in 1992; French paperback edition, center, published in 1994; and German edition, right, published in 1994.

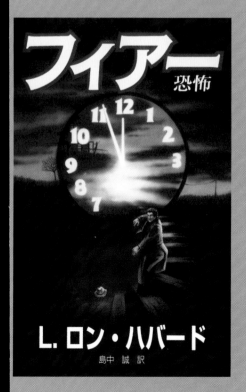

フィアー
恐怖

L. ロン・ハバード
島中 誠 訳

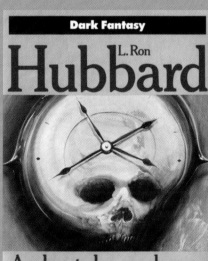

Dark Fantasy

L. Ron
Hubbard

Au bout du cauchemar

Par cette délicieuse journée de prin-temps, dans le bureau du docteur Chalmers, à la clinique du collège d'Atworthy, deux petits esprits de l'air auraient pu être tapis dans

DAS GRAUEN

ROMAN

L. RON HUBBARD

DĚS

NAKLADATELSTVÍ SVOBODA - LIBERTAS

OMNIA

HOROR

L. RON HUBBARD

L. RON HUBBARD
LE QUATTRO ORE
DEL TERRORE

James Lowry ha perso quattro ore della sua vita, sparite chissà come dalla memoria. Quattro ore appena, ma il principio di un incubo che può durare per sempre...
ROMANZO

EDITRICE NORD

L. RON HUBBARD

"A classic tale of creeping, surreal menace and horror... one of the really, really good ones."
—STEPHEN KING

FEAR

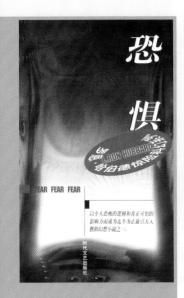

Chinese edition, published in 1997.

Lithuanian edition, published in 1999.

English paperback edition, published in 1998.

A MAN OF MANY NAMES

THE PROLIFIC L. RON HUBBARD WROTE HIS FICTION UNDER at least fifteen pen names, ranging from the martial Winchester Remington Colt to the exotic Rene Lafayette to the bland Ken Martin. While this was sometimes requested by editors when they wanted to publish more than one of his stories in the same magazine issue (which happened often), it was also, Hubbard explained, a device some writers used when editors dropped them because they had become too successful and, thus, too expensive.

Sometimes, in a manner of speaking, these names took on a life of their own, such as the Germanic-sounding Kurt von Rachen. As Hubbard tells it, he wrote a story, "The Squad That Never Came Back," and signed it "Kurt von Rachen." Then he had his agent, Ed Bodin, submit it as a story from a "new" writer to Leo Margulies, editor of *Thrilling Adventures* magazine.

Hubbard explained what happened:

"Ed was scared stiff. 'But if he finds out . . .'

"I pushed him hard. It was a gag on Leo. So Ed did it.

"Day or two later, Ed called me in a panic. 'They love it. But they want to know what this guy looks like.'

"So I said, 'He's a huge brute of a man. Tough. Black hair, beard. His idea of a party is to rent the floor of a hotel, get everybody drunk and smash the place to bits. A tough character.'

"So Ed hung up and all seemed well.

"Then the next day he called again in even more of a panic. 'They want to know where he is! They want to see him! And sign a contract!'

"So I said, 'He's in the Argentine. He's wanted for murder in Georgia!'

"So Ed hung up. All went through smoothly.

"Now it's not illegal to use a pen name. But to play such a joke on an old friend like Leo was bad.

"So I went over to Leo's office to tell him for laughs.

"Unfortunately, Leo met me with a manuscript in his hand.

"He said, 'You old-time pros think you are all there is! Look at this. A story, brand-new, fresh. New writer. Got it all over you.'

"And the manuscript he was holding was 'The Squad That Never Came Back' by 'Kurt von Rachen.'

"I let it go.

"I used the name amongst others for some years. But that isn't all there is to the story.

"After the war years, I was riding down in an elevator in Leo's building. A brand-new fresh writer had stepped in with me.

"'I just sold three stories,' he said.

"I was glad for him. Most pros are for the new ones that are trying.

"'Yeah,' he said, 'and this sure is a *wild* town,' meaning New York. 'Last night I was at a party. Guy rented a whole floor of a hotel, got everybody drunk, smashed the place up . . .'"

"I started, blinked. Could it be?

"'What was his name?' I inquired breathlessly.

"'Kurt von Rachen,' he said. And left me standing there forgetting to get out."

Snake River, Grand Teton National Park in Wyoming, circa 1936.

An alphabetical listing of the pen names used by L. Ron Hubbard for his fiction:

Winchester Remington Colt
Lt. Jonathan Daly
Capt. Charles Gordon
Capt. L. Ron Hubbard
Bernard Hubbel
Michael Keith
Rene Lafayette
Legionnaire 148
Legionnaire 14830
Ken Martin
Scott Morgan
Lt. Scott Morgan
Kurt von Rachen
Barry Randolph
Capt. Humbert Reynolds

OTHER WORLDS

T*ypewriter in the Sky,* the third in the trio of landmarks of
speculative fiction published by L. Ron Hubbard in 1940,
appeared in the November and December issues of *Unknown.*

A richly original story-within-a-story—the tale of an
author and the main character in a novel he's writing locked in a
frantic, funny do-or-die battle of wits and wills—*Typewriter in the
Sky* is one of Hubbard's most enduring works. Like *Fear* and
Final Blackout, it introduced the genre to a new level of creative
invention. And like them, it has resonated across the succeeding

generations of speculative fiction, frequently inspiring imitation in print, on the screen and in the theater. A recent Broadway musical, for example, switched the setting and the characters to Hollywood, but the love-hate duel between the author and his fictional hero remained the production's centerpiece. As author-editor Frederik Pohl confirmed: "Fans and other writers were doing variations on that for years."

In his introduction to *Battlefield Earth*, L. Ron Hubbard observed that, unlike science fiction, "fantasy gives you no limits at all." In *Typewriter in the Sky*, this boundlessness springs exuberantly to life. Mike de Wolf, a dilettante piano player, finds himself stranded in "Blood and Loot," a swashbuckling buccaneer adventure novel—"flashing rapiers, tall ships, brave men"—being written against an inhospitable publishing deadline by his friend, the eminent "fictioneer" Horace Hackett. Not only is Mike de Wolf *in* the novel, but he discovers to his deep dismay that he has been cast as the notorious villain, Miguel de Lobo. Knowing full well that Horace Hackett villains are always fated to die, Mike-as-Miguel plots desperately to save himself and change the outcome of the story. Meanwhile, Horace pounds away on his "typewriter in the sky," littering the old Spanish Main with hilarious anachronisms (Mike plays Mozart on a piano labeled "Steinway, Chicago") and lamenting how characters sometimes take on lives of their own.

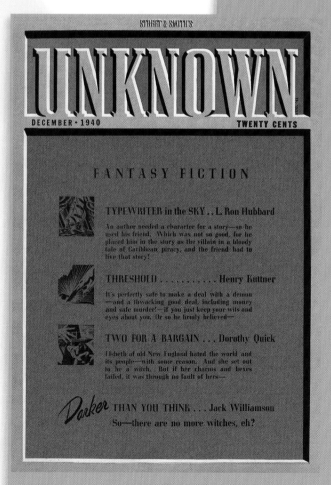

Part 2 of *Typewriter in the Sky*, published in December 1940.

Part 1 of *Typewriter in the Sky* first appeared in November 1940.

Illustrations by Edd Cartier for
Typewriter in the Sky.

English hardcover edition of *Typewriter in the Sky*, center, published in 1995. Italian edition, right, published in 1997.

Hubbard took gleefully inventive liberties with the historic details of the Spanish Main. Indeed, at the time, there was a widely shared view that *Typewriter in the Sky* was a masterly parody of Sabatini's *Sea Hawk* and *Captain Blood* pirate extravaganzas. And it is true that Hubbard certainly knew the Caribbean intimately, both from extensive research and firsthand from his motion-picture and mineralogical journeys of the early 1930s.

Typewriter in the Sky also displays his thorough grasp of nautical detail. There are passages in the novel that recreate life at sea with almost photographic fidelity, drawn from his own South Pacific voyages as a young man and as a youthful helmsman aboard a commercial vessel plying the China Sea. And even as he was writing *Typewriter in the Sky* earlier in 1940, he was preparing for a trip that same summer aboard his sailing vessel *Maggie,* under the Explorers Club flag, to chart the inland passage to Alaska while testing an experimental radio navigational system and studying Indian tribal communities along the way.

Typewriter in the Sky's stature as a creative milestone in the history of fantasy has been undeniable since its debut in *Unknown*. Critics and literary historians regard it as the prototypical "inward voyage" or "journey of the mind" story. Others see its interactive "interior realities" as a pioneering application of "virtual reality" to the storyteller's art in both the "real" world of Horace Hackett's New York City and Mike de Wolf's "virtual" world of the Spanish Main.

Critic and commentator James Gunn has noted that *Typewriter in the Sky* anticipated plot devices now highly popular among many writers. And for science fiction author Kevin J. Anderson, the novel is simply "a true masterpiece of the genre."

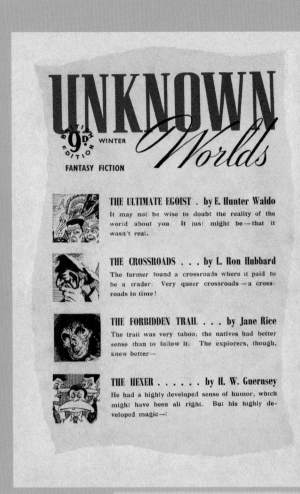

"**The Crossroads**" was first published in February 1941 and later in 1949 in this British edition of *Unknown Worlds*. Illustration by Edd Cartier.

But it was author and editor Damon Knight, in his book *In Search of Wonder* (1967), who found L. Ron Hubbard's imagery, tone and cryptic wit encapsulated in what Knight calls the "three immortal lines" with which the novel ends:

"Abruptly Mike de Wolf stopped. His jaw slacked a trifle and his hand went up to his mouth to cover it. His eyes were fixed upon the fleecy clouds which scurried across the moon.

"Up there—

"God?

"In a dirty bathrobe?"

L. Ron Hubbard's stories continued to appear in *Unknown* and *Astounding Science Fiction* throughout 1941—among them the embattled future of "The Kilkenny Cats," the nexus of time in "The Crossroads," and the errant wizardry of *The Case of the Friendly Corpse.* But by the summer of that year, Hubbard had already been commissioned a lieutenant (jg) in the Navy Reserve, and by early December, with America's entry into the war, he was posted to active duty in Australia and, later, to a sea command in the Pacific theater.

Between January 1942 and April 1943, however, nine more of his stories were published, ranging from the strange, sentient nebula of "The Invaders" and the war with Saturn in "Strain" to the prowling Venusian menace of "The Beast" and the world of the double sun in "The Great Secret." The latter would, in fact, be his last published story until 1947 when, with the war and its painful physical aftermath behind him, he would return to the world of fiction with a vital new surge of creative energy to produce the grand cosmos of "Ole Doc Methuselah," the remote future of "The Conquest of Space" series, the powerful *The End Is Not Yet,* and the groundbreaking *To the Stars.*

Hubbard's first postwar story in July 1947 was, however, not science fiction or fantasy. It was "The Chee-Chalker," a tough-edged mystery-adventure-romance with unexplained deaths, drug smugglers and a missing government cop. "The Chee-Chalker" emphatically announced to the readers of *Five Novels Monthly,* and to the world, that a first-rate storyteller was back. Even as the pulp era was beginning to fade, a victim, finally, of television and the emergence of the paperback, Hubbard would produce forty-seven more adventure, western, mystery and speculative fiction stories and novels in the next three years.

The End Is Not Yet, Part 1, appeared in August 1947. Cover art by Hubert Rogers.

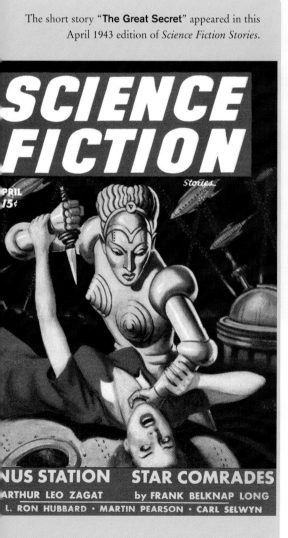

The short story "**The Great Secret**" appeared in this April 1943 edition of *Science Fiction Stories.*

Among the forty-seven final works was *The End Is Not Yet,* marking his return to science fiction and fantasy in the August, September and October 1947 issues of *Astounding.* A vast, compelling history of another "future" America on another parallel time plane born in a shattering instant of atomic fury, *The End Is Not Yet* sweeps across continents and through wars of desolation. Then, in the wake of nuclear devastation, physicist Charles Martel and an unlikely assortment of scientists, convicts and soldiers band together to topple the global empire of the most ruthless man alive, Axel Werner.

Hubbard startles and engrosses us from the very beginning—a slow "grayish murk of fog" cloaks what is really a bridge in time and space. The seemingly substantial figure of a Columbia University professor who crosses the bridge proves suddenly to be an insubstantial hologram, a visionary concept in 1947. And the biography of the Charles Martel of that world, delivered by the hologram "professor" to the counterpart Martel of this world, becomes, finally, the body of the novel itself.

The End Is Not Yet powerfully develops a number of Hubbard's most treasured ideals—courage, freedom, the responsibilities of leadership and the buoyant hope for a future he measures lyrically in the closing lines of the novel: "Why, we are writers and singers of songs. And have to do with beauty and laughter."

The first of the "Ole Doc Methuselah" stories appeared with Edd Cartier illustrations in the October 1947 issue of *Astounding.* These tales of a space voyaging medical knight-errant—one of a select society of six hundred Soldier of Light immortals in selfless galactic service to mankind—and his multiarmed alien companion, Hippocrates, would dazzle readers for years to come.

But with the conclusion of *The End Is Not Yet* running prominently in the same October issue under the Hubbard byline, John Campbell wanted to avoid creating the impression that one writer dominated the entire magazine. So, the pen name Rene Lafayette—one which had appeared seven years earlier on *The Indigestible Triton*—was resurrected and affixed to "Ole Doc Methuselah."

The result was remarkable. Campbell later reported that L. Ron Hubbard had, indeed, successfully competed with—and bested—himself in the magazine's reader-response poll: Lafayette's "Ole Doc Methuselah" was voted the most popular story in *Astounding*'s October issue, with Hubbard's *The End Is Not Yet* placing just behind it, in second. Over the next three years, when Rene Lafayette would also become the signature for "The Conquest of Space" series in *Startling Stories*—even as the "Ole Doc Methuselah" stories continued to appear in *Astounding*—the pen name would take on a status and identity distinctly, and enduringly, of its own.

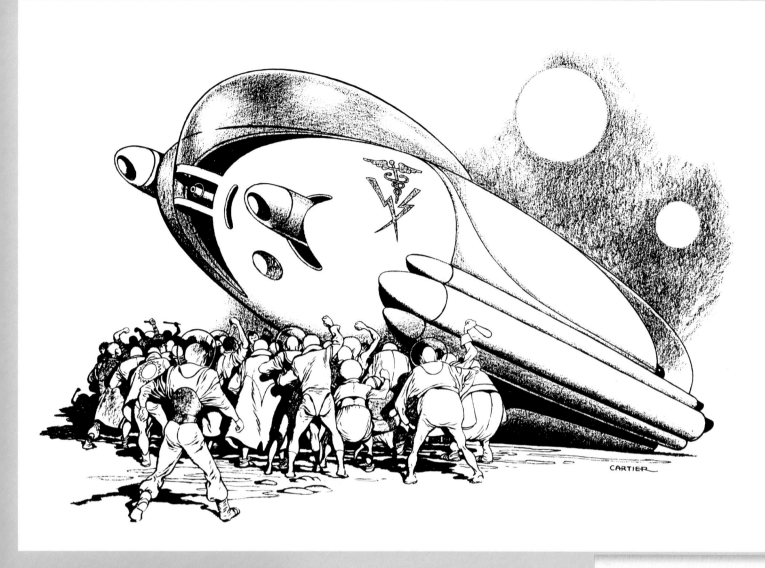

"**Ole Doc Methuselah**," the first story in the series of the same name, was written under the pen name Rene Lafayette and first published in October 1947. Cover art by Chesley Bonestell and illustrations by Edd Cartier. Also appearing in this same issue was the third part and conclusion to Hubbard's story *The End Is Not Yet*.

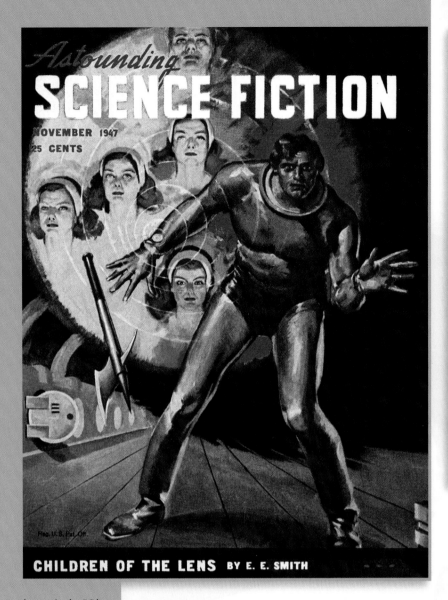

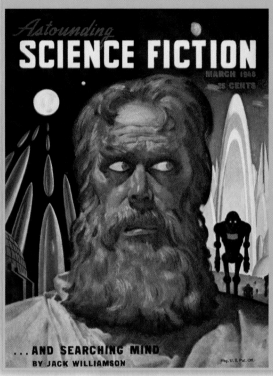

Astounding published seven "Ole Doc Methuselah" stories in all, culminating with "Ole Mother Methuselah" in January 1950. Their popularity was immediate and their acknowledgment as a golden age classic has never waned. Ole Doc—his real name was Stephen Thomas Methridge, M.D., Johns Hopkins, '46—and his bookish, gypsum-eating colleague roamed the intergalactic starways, battling skulduggery, injustice and disease. Their journeys range with resourceful good humor across an immense galactic universe, from the swindler planet Spico in the opening story, through the extortionate tax on breathable air in "The Great Air Monopoly," to the troublesome superhumans of "Ole Mother Methuselah."

The action is fast and exhilarating, but, beyond that, the stories also embody what author and editor Robert Silverberg has called breathless inventiveness and a rich sense of wonder. It is true: they present that seismic moment of discovery in science fiction when the reader knows with certainty that he or she has experienced something unexpected but momentously possible.

"**Plague!**" the fifth in the "Ole Doc Methuselah" series, published in April 1949.

Astounding

SCIENCE FICTION

Reg. U. S. Pat. Off.

APRIL 1949
25 CENTS

PLAGUE!
BY RENE LAFAYETTE

SANTRY

Astounding
SCIENCE FICTION ®

SEPTEMBER 1948
25 CENTS

"A Sound Investment," sixth in the "Ole Doc Methuselah" series, was published in the June 1949 issue of *Astounding Science Fiction* Cover art by Chesley Bonestell.

Astounding
SCIENCE FICTION

JUNE 1949
25 CENTS

THE APHRODITE PROJECT BY PHILIP LATHAM

"The Great Air Monopoly," the fourth story in the "Ole Doc Methuselah" series, was published in September 1948. Cover art by Chesley Bonestell and illustrations by Edd Cartier.

"**Ole Mother Methuselah,**" the seventh and last in the "Ole Doc Methuselah" series, appeared in this January 1950 issue of *Astounding Science Fiction*. Cover art by Chesley Bonestell and interior illustrations by Edd Cartier.

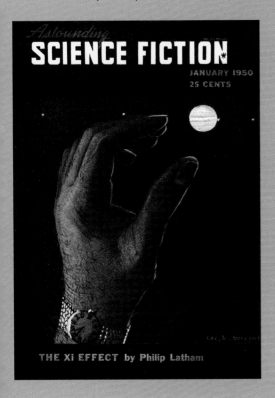

WORKING WITH L. RON HUBBARD

by Edd Cartier

L. RON HUBBARD AND I FIRST MET IN EDITOR JOHN W. CAMPBELL'S OFFICE at the Street & Smith building in Manhattan. Except for an occasional meeting in that office, at a lunch, and at a few science fiction conventions, my contact with Ron was through his manuscripts. With the advent of the fantasy pulp *Unknown,* it did not take long before Campbell was publishing a lot of Ron's work and I was given the opportunity to depict much of it. I illustrated more stories by Hubbard than for any other author during my years of work for both *Unknown* and *Astounding Science Fiction.*

Illustrating Ron's tales was a welcome assignment because they always contained scenes or incidents I found easy to picture. With some writers' work I sometimes had to contact Campbell for an idea. That never happened with a Hubbard story. His plots allowed my imagination to run wild and the ideas for my illustrations would quickly come to mind.

Hubbard's work for *Unknown* was well suited to the magazine and to my style. Campbell made a special point of letting me illustrate Ron's stories. They offered fantastic opportunities to draw blustering, swaggering heroes and wickedly depraved villains. In the novels *Slaves of Sleep* and *Typewriter in the Sky* Ron gave free rein to the swashbuckling, historically costumed characters I loved to sketch. I was able to fill my illustrations with humorously grotesque faces and to add atmosphere with old guns, burning candles, rope and swords. Ron's other novels in *Unknown* allowed me to depict my visions of his ghouls, devils, demons and old hags. Those type of ghastly characters in *Death's Deputy, Fear* and *The Case of the Friendly Corpse* were among my specialties. I relished the chance to draw them and often enjoyed adding a smile or hint of humor to their gruesomeness.

Though I painted only a handful of covers for the pulps, two of them happened to be for Hubbard's novels *Death's Deputy* and *The Indigestible Triton,* when they appeared in *Unknown.* Both paintings were done in oils. The devil on the cover for *Death's Deputy* seemed to be a favorite with many readers. The strong orange and red colors of the illustration stood out quite well at the newsstands, but caused some people to describe *Unknown*'s covers as lurid. Their complaints about it and other paintings of a similar sort soon led to the end of the magazine's full-colored cover illustrations. They were replaced by a very conservative listing of contents described as "dignified" by Campbell. Unfortunately, the change took place just before Ron's novel *Fear* was published. What a cover I could have done for that tale; lurid, yes, but in a dark and menacing way that would have only hinted at the violence revealed in the story's climax. Indeed, much of Ron's work for *Unknown* was of the fearsome, haunting vein that I delighted in illustrating.

Campbell had me illustrate Hubbard's "Ole Doc Methuselah" for a 1947 issue of *Astounding*. That short story was the beginning of the famous series about Ole Doc, Hippocrates, and their stellar travels on behalf of the Universal Medical Society. I worked on quite a few of Ron's stories for *Astounding*, but it was Ole Doc's adventures that many people, including myself, recall most fondly. Readers liked my depiction of Hippocrates and I always enjoyed drawing the little, antennaed, four-armed creature. Oddly enough, in 1952 my wife, Gina, found a large five-legged frog in our yard. The extraordinary coincidence of the frog's arrival and my illustration of Hippocrates still astounds me. Needless to say, the mutant frog was instantly dubbed Hippocrates or Pocrates, for short. He resided with honor in a garden pool and was featured in many local newspaper articles. The frog's existence was as if Ron's writings and my illustrations had come to life to prove that science fiction's imaginative ideas are quite within the realm of possibility.

In a letter to me, L. Ron Hubbard once wrote, "Thanks for Ole Doc, my talented cohort. Your Hippocrates is just plain wonderful." To me, it was wonderful that our work together complemented each other's abilities, enhanced our reputations, and brought a large measure of enjoyment to the readers of fantasy and science fiction. Ron and I could not have hoped for much more than that.

—*Edd Cartier*

THE CONQUEST OF SPACE

In the introduction to *Battlefield Earth*, L. Ron Hubbard recalls a now legendary meeting "of old scientist and science-fiction friends" he attended in 1945, in the very infancy of the Space Age. "The meeting was at the home of my dear friend, the incomparable Bob Heinlein. And do you know what was their agenda? How to get man into space fast enough so that he would be distracted from further wars on Earth."

It was, indeed, a greater vision of man in space, of the stars as mankind's destination, and, intrinsically, of science fiction as the imaginative catalyst for the journey, that L. Ron Hubbard brought to his "Conquest of Space" future history series. Preceded thematically by the much anthologized "When Shadows Fall"—with its haunting opening line, "There came a day when Earth lay dying, for planets also die"—this series of nine linked stories appeared in *Startling Stories* under the Rene Lafayette pen name from January 1949 to the last in the series, "Tough Old Man," in November 1950.

"The Conquest of Space" series—much like the earlier "Kilkenny Cats" and the contemporaneous "Ole Doc Methuselah" stories—inspired intense reader enthusiasm. Again, the letters to *Startling Stories* became the best calibration of the series' popularity, from the relative restraint of the West Virginia reader who called it "the best that has appeared in [*Startling Stories*] in the past seven years," to one that applauded it as "the best you have ever published!" to the reader from New York City who simply said, "More, and more, and more is all we can ask."

Each "Conquest of Space" story had its individuality. January 1949's "Forbidden Voyage," about an early space explorer whose pioneering trip to the Moon remains in complete obscurity, was hailed by a young reader named Marion Zimmer as "the type of thing we need more of in modern stf." That's "scientifiction," which still enjoyed a substantial currency at the time as a descriptive for the genre. The following year, however, it was as Marion Zimmer Bradley—later the author of *The Mists of Avalon* and other books—that she characterized "The Last Admiral" and its suicide mission against the first pirate colony in space as "the finest story you have printed in many and many a day!"

There were other "Conquest of Space" stories that were equally well received. Two in particular endure as favorites: the riveting "Beyond the Black Nebula," about a man who must cross the forbidden Coal Sack nebula to retrieve his devastated reputation, and the thoughtfully diverting "Emperor of the Universe," about a space-roving "Johnny Appleseed" and his true mission as a pathfinder to the stars.

Even as "The Conquest of Space" and the "Ole Doc Methuselah" series were appearing in parallel in *Startling Stories* and *Astounding Science Fiction*, however, Hubbard's creative energies were producing a remarkable array of other stories. Under his own name and as Rene Lafayette, for magazines ranging from *Astounding* and *Startling Stories* to *Thrilling Wonder* and *Super Science*, these tales have remained fixed in the canon of modern speculative fiction. There's the lively dilemma of the unwary real estate investor who buys a planet on which he can't sit down in "A Matter of Matter"; the special-effects racehorse—straight out of Hubbard's Hollywood period as a screenwriter—whose construction conceals a secret space project, in the farcically delightful *The Automagic Horse;* the re-emergence of Sleepy McGee (from the "Hell Job" stories of 1936) as an engineer

the incredible destination

James Dolan's heroic route to the stars was centuries old before man in his ignorance was permitted to journey thereon!

by RENE LaFAYETTE

AMONG the many tales of the early voyagers of space, the story of James Dolan should rank high. It did not at the time. It was not even known for five hundred years and then it was received as like a hoax for the curious items in the almanac. James Dolan, as a name, is lost in the modern history book. For five centuries it was synonymous with charlatan, for in those distant days when man was fixated on his birth planet, Earth, he came to believe very little of what he was told about space. Five headed dwarfs and nine-tailed dogs "from Venus" had too often been shown in side-shows.

Space travel, in the vernacular, was a flop. Seventy-five years after the first voyages the botanical system in vogue did not fret about survival expansion. It concentrated on such things as food production and birth control

and although here and there men dreamed about future sovereignty of the universe, the mass opinion was opposed. It is very difficult to overcome the inertia of a government or a people. They had Mars. It cost seventeen thousand dollars to transport one man and his baggage to that apparently worthless sphere and the men who had that kind of money had, in the main, no reason to risk their lives going off to a frontier. Only one ship in eight arrived. The return cargo was of small value.

Jupiter, Saturn, Venus and the rest had little to offer an Earthman. The violent fate of the U. S. Jupiter Survey Expedition, the tales of cannibalism in it, the incredible agonies of its members for space travel lack many, many years. They had not properly prepared and that, in an expedition, is fatal to more than the one voyage.

The third in a series on the Conquest of Space

Illustration from "**The Incredible Destination**," as it appeared in *Startling Stories*, May 1949.

forbidden voyag

George Carlyle knew the way to get to the Moon—but the conscientious folk in authority did their best to block his path!

Illustration from "**The Unwilling Hero**," from *Startling Stories*, July 1949.

Illustration from "**Forbidden Voyage**," from *Startling Stories*, January 1949. The first in a series on "The Conquest of Space," stories written under the pen name of Rene Lafayette.

the unwilling hero

No hunger for personal glory lured Vic Hardin into the reaches of outer space on a daring rescue mission— he was ordered out there by his editor!

by RENE LaFAYETTE

TEN of thousands of years ago, Earth and Earthmen had no concept of the stars nor the destiny of mankind. Difficult as it may be to believe, the tiny planet which gave birth to Barstow, Chun-Ka, Vhtlow and Marin looked upon space travel and conquest as a sort of novelty, a thing to be read about in the Sunday Feature Section, a stunt without any great meaning or scope.

The average Earthman thought such voyages vaguely interesting but of no personal concern to himself. Expeditions, he believed,

went out to help astronomers and check their guesses, to collect new animals for the zoo or provide heroes for parades up Fifth Avenue.

According to the records which exist in the Galactic Archives (exhumed lately from a ruined library on Mars) Victor Hughes Hardin—*the* V. H. Hardin so dear to legend—had no more idea of being a space explorer before he became one, than he had of being immortal.

The school children who dutifully chant

One of a series of stories on the Conquest of Space

by RENE LaFAYETTE

INTRODUCTION: It would seem at this far distant time that the literature of Mankind, embellished as it is by thousands of names, by trillions of books by title in hundreds of millions of libraries throughout width and depth of space, might still furnish some small volume which would give, in human style of the acts themselves, a read-account of Man's Conquest of Space.

Today, sitting smugly on his thousands of [...], protected and served by a hundred [millen]iums of experience, Man takes history for granted and pays never a bow to those resounding names which composited his Destiny. And if he thinks of them at all, shuttling safely across a million light years of space, it is to dismiss them for it is so easy now.

But what high courage it must have taken for Man to launch his projects into the mystery of space, for he had no answer to a hundred million intricate problems, any one of which might well snuff out his life. What courage he showed and how dauntless must have been his spirit!

The first in a series on the Conquest of Space

Illustration from "**Beyond the Black Nebula**," which appeared in the September 1949 issue of *Startling Stories*.

beyond the black nebula

Oddly, Anthony Twain could cleanse his blackened name only by crossing the sky's darkest blot—the strange and dreaded Coal Sack!

by RENE LaFAYETTE

IN the early days of space exploration, the name of Anthony Twain was synonymous with adventure, dash and daring. For forty years—a long time even in that fast moving epoch—the face and fame of this man dazzled the people of Earth and drove them on and ever on toward new goals of accomplishment in the conquering of All.

And yet there was a time when the mention of Anthony Twain brought laughter in any gathering and ridicule in print. That was the time that our histories have forgotten about, our folk songs never mention. But it was a time which may come to any man. Anthony Twain became old, a has-been.

Actually, he was never an explorer at all. He had been on two fortuitous trips—adventure enough in those ancient days when a ten-light-year speed was considered impossible and space vessels fell apart in collision with the meanest meteorite—and he had prospered through his writings.

He had the gift of color and drama, the flamboyance and the flare which the public in any time has adored. But he had not done anything.

An explorer might be great in the annals of the Explorer's Club and the files of the Extra-Terrestrial Department of Earth. But he did not become known to the public un-

A story in the series on the Conquest of Space!

Illustration from "**The Emperor of the Universe**," from *Startling Stories*, November 1949.

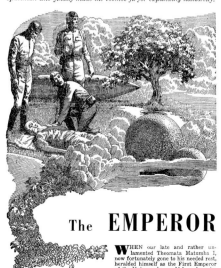

A Story in the Series on the Conquest of Space

From a far-distant future is recorded the legend of the half-crazed spaceman who finally made the cosmos fit for expanding humanity!

by RENE LaFAYETTE

We gave him a fine funeral and a cairn of stone

The EMPEROR of the UNIVERSE

WHEN our late and rather unlamented Theomata Matumba I, now fortunately gone to his needed rest, heralded himself as the First Emperor of the Universe he would have been indignant and amazed to find that he was wrong. The First Emperor of the Universe lived, ruled and died about an hundred millenia ago.

The archives at New Earth, lately exhumed by the Galactic Archeological Society, contained an infinity of data about our forebears not hitherto known. As neither Theomata Matumba I nor his profligate courtiers inclined much, it appears, to the scholarly horizons, they probably missed with many others the paper written on the subject by Dr. Perault of the Carlyle System Bibliotech.

However it was probably just as well,

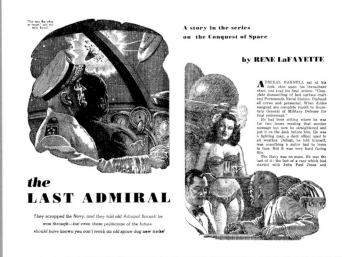

with cosmic challenges in "The Planet Maker"; and the sudden, breath-catching pause (it's like having the air sucked out of a room, a reader said) when the dark identity of "the Arbiter" is finally revealed in *The Kingslayer*.

Then, in the December 1949 issue of *Astounding*, John Campbell notified his readers that the magazine would publish "a new, remarkably powerful novel" by L. Ron Hubbard, starting in February of the following year. He repeated the announcement in January 1950 (the issue in which "Ole Doc Methuselah" ended its run in *Astounding* with Rene Lafayette at his virtuoso best in "Ole Mother Methuselah"), promising again that the upcoming Hubbard novel would be "a two-parter, and a beautiful development of the theme based on the time-rate differential of ships traveling near the speed of light."

That novel, *To the Stars,* met and exceeded Campbell's promise. It is quintessential science fiction, a story of cosmic dimensions built with masterly skill from hard, scientific theory—in this case, the Einstein–Lorentz-Fitzgerald "time-dilation" equation:

"As mass approaches the speed of light, time approaches zero."

Hubbard initially encountered the theory as an engineering student at George Washington University and first broached the equation as a theme in his story "Beyond All Weapons" in the January issue of *Super Science Stories*. In *To the Stars,* the motif took on groundbreaking proportions—a story seminal in scope, technical detail and influence and, by reader and critical consensus, the classic science fiction treatment of the time-dilation effect.

The novel opens with one of the most celebrated—and reverberantly powerful—first lines in the history of the genre:

"Space is deep, Man is small and Time is his relentless enemy."

The crew of the spaceship *Hound of Heaven* are rootless exiles aboard a pariah ship, from an Earth and a generation that has grown old and passed on even as they remain essentially untouched by the relative time of what Hubbard evocatively calls "a cold equation, a dispassionate mathematics . . . [a] sentence to forever." Alan Corday, a young engineer, is shanghaied by the *Hound*'s inscrutably aloof Captain Duard Henry Jocelyn, to be trained, for reasons Corday does not understand, to succeed Jocelyn as commander. When he does, in fact, become captain of the *Hound of Heaven,* Corday embarks on a new journey described for us in a final paragraph Campbell lauded for its crystallizing brevity:

"And high into the black, black void the *Hound of Heaven* sped, upward bound and outward bound on a mission to the ageless stars."

To the Stars was voted the top story in the issue by *Astounding*'s reader-response poll and praised for its power, the depth and range of its characterization, and "its solidity of ideas."

It has since been published in many other countries, usually under the title *Return to Tomorrow*—*Ritorno al Domani* in Italian, *Retour à Demain* in French, *Återkomst till Morgondagen* in Swedish, for example. And, indisputably, *To the Stars* remains the trendsetting story of its kind in the genre and an engrossing and defining classic.

Three years earlier, L. Ron Hubbard had sounded a theme of telling importance in a passage in *The End Is Not Yet*.

"The only valuable thing on earth—and never forget this—is the mind of man," he wrote. "With that mind can be produced everything else. . . .

"And the only valuable thing to a man is his own dignity, his freedom. . . ."

Though necessarily expressed with narrative succinctness, the ideas were large and compelling. They, indeed, reflected the sense of the original research into the human mind and spirit Hubbard had intensively pursued for many years and for which his immense literary production had provided both the freedom and financial wherewithal. Now, with the fruition of that research embodied in the landmark publication in 1950 of his *Dianetics: The Modern Science of Mental Health,* he embarked on three decades of writing and lecturing voluminously on the mind and spirit. Though he remained in touch throughout those years with many of his colleagues from the golden age, including John Campbell, A.E. van Vogt and Robert Heinlein, he politely but persistently declined when urged to return to the field of fiction and, particularly, to the genre upon which he had left such a deep and abiding mark.

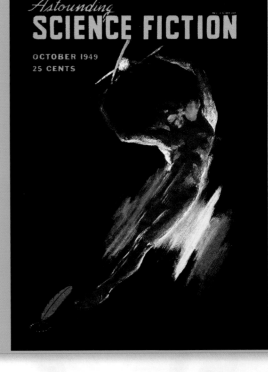

The *Automagic Horse* first appeared in this October 1949 issue with original illustrations by Edd Cartier.

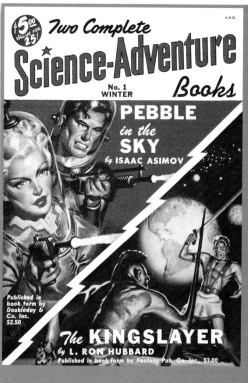

To the Stars, entitled *Return to Tomorrow* in Italian, published in 1995.

Original cover of *To the Stars*, February 1950. Cover art by Hubert Rogers.

Illustrated hardcover edition of *The Automagic Horse*, published in 1994. Cover art and illustrations by Scott E. Sutton.

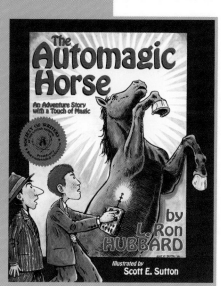

The Kingslayer, published in the winter of 1950.

BATTLEFIELD EARTH

R ecently there came a period when I had little to do. This was novel in a life so crammed with busy years, and I decided to amuse myself by writing a novel that was *pure* science fiction."

These whimsically unassuming opening words of L. Ron Hubbard's introduction to 1982's *Battlefield Earth* are deceptively revealing. The novel is pure science fiction, but of monumental breadth and creative vision. It is also a classic of storytelling and a literary beacon because of its revitalizing influence on the scope and popularity of the genre.

Freed of the arbitrary restraints of the old magazine format, Hubbard rolled out the biggest single science fiction novel ever

ROBERT A. HEINLEIN   6000 BONNY DOON ROAD   CALIFORNIA 95060

SANTA CRUZ COUNTY

16 Dec 1982

L. Ron Hubbard
Post Office Box 29550
Los Angeles, CA 90029

Dear Ron,

BATTLEFIELD EARTH is a terrific story!

It puts me in mind of FINAL BLACKOUT in its flavor, but with this difference: It is a much more complex story with more characters drawn in full, a much longer story and one that, by being longer, has room enough for you to treat far more subjects in depth--serious subjects worthy of thorough treatment.

It was a good story from page one, then it got better when we reached Scotland, then still better in Africa, then again when ships from other cultures showed up, then (for my taste) reached its high point, and stayed there, when you revealed that the little gray men were intergalactic bankers.

The carefully underplayed comedy you made of this development I found delicious.

The only criticism that I have of this book is that it is just too heavy and bulky to read comfortably in bed. Next time, can you manage to hold yourself down to 100- to 150,000 words at a time?

It's a great story, Ron. I hope it sells a million copies in hard back. It tickles me enormously to see you turn out such a masterpiece in your seventieth year--it makes these "new wave" writers who can't write English and don't know science (or much of anything else) look silly.

No special news here--back from one trip, getting ready for another, and swamped in paper work. But both of us in good heatlh--no complaints, Sergeant! I am fiddling around with my latest novel, trying to get back into it. I have been away from it too long--a mistake for a writer with a lifetime habit of writing a book the way most writers write a short story, right straight through and don't stop for anything. I think you write that way, too, but most of our colleagues piddle around with a book over a long period of time--or so I hear.

Again let me say how much I enjoyed BATTLEFIELD EARTH.

Always your friend,

Robert A. Heinlein

published—428,750 words across more than a thousand pages. But it is larger than its mere size. *Battlefield Earth* is panoramic in concept, style and execution. By every measure it is an adventure of epic dimensions, a Saga of the Year 3000, a novel of an apocalyptic future in which mankind has been conquered and all but annihilated, its survivors brutalized for a millennium by an alien colossus.

If *Battlefield Earth* is a masterwork of pure science fiction, it is also, as Hubbard reminds us, "the herald of possibility." With a vital sense of wonder drawn from the plausible, rather than from fantasy, it is neither a snapshot of a scene nor a sketch of a moment. It is an engrossing, fully textured palette of the genres in which Hubbard had achieved such prominence during the pulp era. "This novel," he wrote, "contains practically every type of story there is—detective, spy, adventure, western, love, air war, you name it." He added one thing

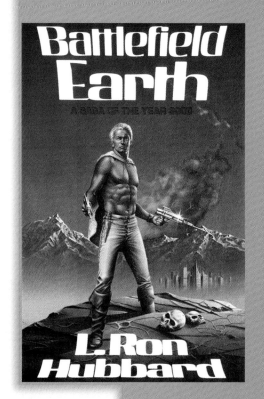

First hardcover edition, 1982.
Cover art by Paul Stinson.

"*Battlefield Earth* is a voluminous work. Well-written. Hubbard really brings characters to life. His action leads to more action and keeps you reading."

—Dr. Yoji Kondo

"*Battlefield Earth* is great fun. It is a non-stop, compelling read. Once you start, you won't be able to put it down."

—Dean Wesley Smith

"*If you like . . . fast, unrelenting* Raiders of the Lost Ark *action, then this is the book for you. It's a real page turner.*"

—Rocky Mountain News

more to the novel's immense narrative range: "The term 'science' also includes economics and sociology and medicine where these are related to material things. So they're in here, too."

Battlefield Earth, of course, signaled L. Ron Hubbard's return—after an absence of three decades of extensive research, writing and lecturing about the human mind and the spiritual nature of man—to popular literature generally and, specifically, to speculative fiction, whose modern form and dimensions he was instrumental in defining. It marked, as well, another period of extraordinary literary production that may be difficult to comprehend, but is impossible to ignore. With *Battlefield Earth,* Hubbard unleashed a torrent of creative vitality, innovation and sheer imaginative audacity that would produce close to two million words of best-selling and influential fiction in only two years.

Battlefield Earth, Hubbard tells us in his retrospective introduction, is the only novel he ever wrote "just to amuse myself." It was also the project he undertook to celebrate his fiftieth year as a professional writer.

Written with a phenomenal burst of creative energy in a sustained eight-month period in 1980, and first published in October 1982, *Battlefield Earth* became a breakaway *New York Times* and international bestseller. It also met with wide critical acclaim evident in such notices as "Writer Resumes Career With Masterful Epic," "A Gripping Thriller of Gargantuan Proportions," and "A True Publishing Event."

Battlefield Earth is towering in scale, in the intensity of its action and tempo, and in the swift interplay of its richly crowded gallery of characters. Its ominous opening line joins the list of other memorably succinct L. Ron Hubbard starts— "Man," said Terl, "is an endangered species."

"Over 1,000 pages of thrills, spills, vicious aliens and noble humans. I found **Battlefield Earth** un-put-downable."

—Neil Gaiman

"**Battlefield Earth** is like a 12-hour 'Indiana Jones' marathon. Non-stop and fast-paced. Every chapter has a big bang-up adventure."

—Kevin J. Anderson

"Pure science fiction… 430,000 words written by a super-writer of the Golden Age of Science Fiction…the great pulp music in every line…will be talked about for a decade… wonderful adventure…great characters…a masterpiece."

—A.E. van Vogt

Gold Mining Disaster
Artist: John Stewart
"Jonnie gazed with horror into the deep canyon. There was a flying drill platform down there, close to the river, and it was in real trouble."

Robert the Fox   Artist: Corey Wolfe
"A grizzled council member stood forward and the chief recognized him as Robert the Fox."

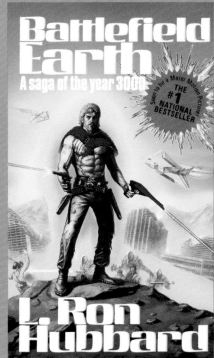

Jonnie Goodboy Tyler
*"Sooner or later someone was bound to rid the galaxies of Psychlo.
Whole races have dreamed that dream."*
This fine illustration is the cover art for the international editions
of **Battlefield Earth**. With art direction by L. Ron Hubbard himself,
it was executed by artist Gerry Grace.

In the year A.D. 3000, Earth is a barren wasteland, plundered of its natural resources by the millennium-long regime of taloned, gas-breathing, nine-foot alien conquerors from the planet Psychlo. Fewer than thirty-five thousand humans survive in a handful of communities scattered across the face of Earth. From one of these, a primitive enclave in the Rocky Mountains near what once was Denver, Colorado, a resourceful young man named Jonnie Goodboy Tyler embarks on a classic hero's journey to challenge the fearful myths of his people. Enslaved by

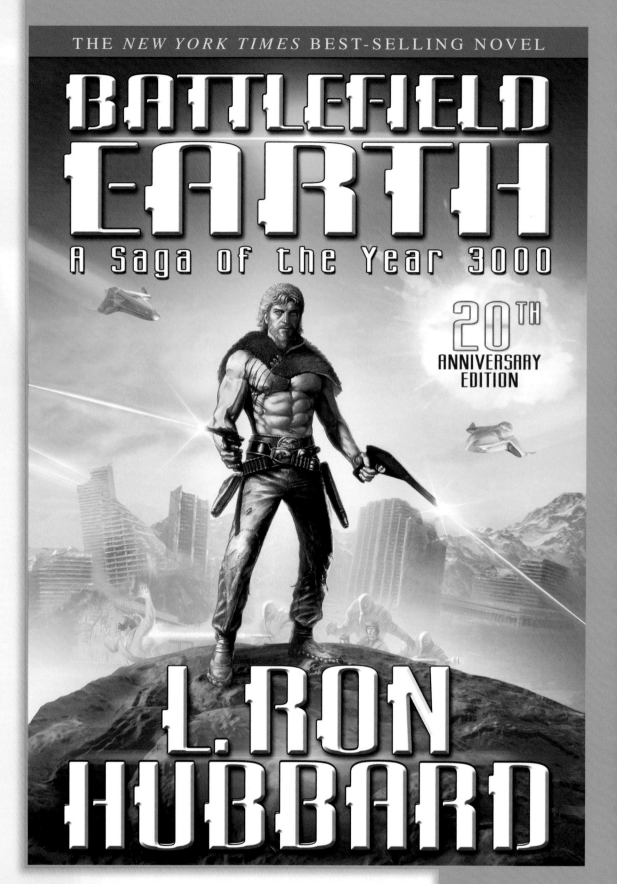

THE *NEW YORK TIMES* BEST-SELLING NOVEL

BATTLEFIELD EARTH
A Saga of the Year 3000

20TH ANNIVERSARY EDITION

L. RON HUBBARD

20th Anniversary hardcover edition, published in 2002.

"This has everything: suspense, pathos, politics, war, humor, diplomacy and intergalactic finance."

—Publishers Weekly

*"Think of the Star Wars sagas, and Raiders of the Lost Ark, mix in the triumph of Rocky I, Rocky II, and Rocky III and you have captured the exuberance, style and glory of **Battlefield Earth**."*

—Baltimore Evening Sun

Pursuit   Artist: Shun Kijima
*"The thing was roaring down the side path behind him.
Now it was turning.... There it was, wisps of smoke
coming out of its nostrils."*

Windsplitter   Artist: Jim Warren
*"Windsplitter came home. He was
on the plain below the pass."*

man's cruelest tormentor, Terl, the Psychlo Security Chief of Earth, Jonnie and a small band of survivors pit their quest for freedom against Terl's ruthless ambition for personal wealth and power in a rebellion that erupts across the continents of Earth and the cosmic sprawl of the Psychlo empire, with the fate of the world, of mankind and of the galaxies beyond in the balance.

The suspense and sheer narrative force of *Battlefield Earth* is breathtaking. "Provocative imagining about the future of the universe," one reviewer said, calibrating the novel's scale, then adding that the novel "is a grand, multi-colored fireworks display of talent that sparkles in style, plot and action." For another critic, the perspective was wide and compelling: "An intergalactic adventure with the imagery and impact of *Star Wars* and a plot that sets it apart as a masterpiece." Echoing L. Ron Hubbard's introductory definition of *Battlefield Earth* as both pure science fiction and a harvest of other genres, the publishing industry's most distinguished magazine, *Publishers Weekly,* applauded Ron's "total mastery of plot and pacing" in crafting the novel and then noted that "This has everything: suspense, pathos, politics, war, humor, diplomacy and intergalactic finance."

Any synopsis of such a grand-scale epic necessarily fails to capture the essence of the endeavor. A plot summary cannot do justice to the imaginative diversity of the novel's characters and alien races, of its military artifacts and striking technologies, or to what one reviewer called the simple magic of *Battlefield Earth*. There is no way to

Chinese edition.

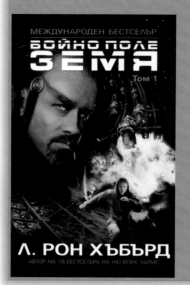

Bulgarian and Korean editions.

SINCE ITS RELEASE, *Battlefield Earth* HAS BEEN published internationally in twenty-five languages: *Brazilian Portuguese, Bulgarian, Chinese, Czech, Danish, Dutch, English, Estonian, French, German, Hebrew, Hungarian, Indonesian, Italian, Japanese, Korean, Lithuanian, Polish, Portuguese, Russian, Serbo-Croatian, Spanish, Swedish, Taiwanese and Turkish.*

offer an adequate miniature sketch of the quick-witted Jonnie Goodboy Tyler, an L. Ron Hubbard protagonist in the heroic mold of the Lieutenant of *Final Blackout* or Charles Martel of *The End Is Not Yet*. Even the *Baltimore Sun*'s description of Jonnie's malevolent adversary, Terl, as "the most deliciously despicable villain of all time" fails to convey the depths of the character or the novel's full dimensions.

There is also a nearly endless cavalcade of alien races marching spectacularly—and often menacingly—through the novel: the hapless Boxnards; the filament-thin Chinko culturalists; the wood-eating Chatovarians and their seven-hundred-planet empire; the incredibly strong Tolneps with their deadly bite and strange infrared vision; and finally, detailed by Hubbard with stinging irony, the Selachee intergalactic bankers, whose financial resources fuel the Psychlo war machine. Inhabitants of a water planet, gray hued, with gill-like appurtenances, upturned noses and double rows of teeth, the Selachee bankers resemble nothing less than sharks.

Finally, there are the dazzling technologies of *Battlefield Earth*, extrapolated from Hubbard's own background, and embodying, again, the central thesis of his introduction—that "Science fiction does *not* come after the fact of a scientific discovery or development. It is the herald of possibility. It is the plea that someone should work on the future."

Of the many developments envisioned by L. Ron Hubbard two decades ago in *Battlefield Earth,* three in particular appear to have taken on substantive relevance in the twenty-first century. Adjustable-frequency "button" cameras—conceptually akin to today's tiny wireless video cameras—are used by the Psychlos to conduct covert surveillance. Camera-like "picto-recorders"—a prescient approximation of digital cameras—are used by the Psychlos to record motion pictures onto disks for instant playback. There are also "atmosphere projectors"—not unlike the remote-sensing space satellites now in use by the United States for intelligence gathering—employed by surviving earthlings to acquire detailed images over vast distances of the unmourned death of the Psychlos' Imperial City.

Finally, there is the technology of teleportation—the instantaneous transfer of matter—the secret of Psychlo invincibility. Teleportation is a recurring theme of Hubbard's fiction, appearing, in one form or another, in "The Dangerous Dimension," "The Tramp," *The End Is Not Yet* and elsewhere. What is most striking, however, about his theoretical speculations is that physicists at such schools as Denmark's University of Aarhus and Australia's National University have reported successful experiments transporting matter—in one case a laser beam of light—instantaneously, from one place to another. The phenomenon, the physicists have explained, is known as teleportation.

The release of *Battlefield Earth* was, as one critic put it, nothing less than a publishing phenomenon that re-energized science fiction as a best-selling mainstream

Estonian, German and Italian editions.

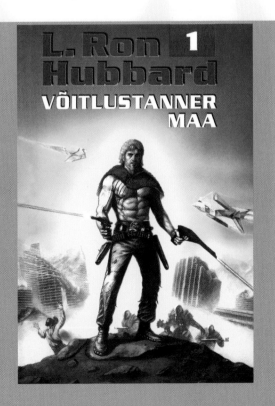

Czech edition.

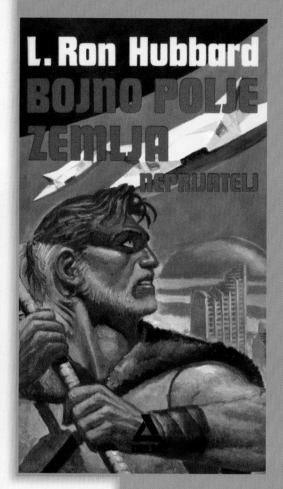

Serbo-Croatian edition.

Danish edition.

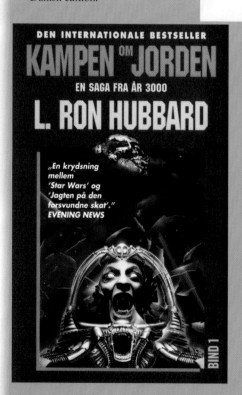

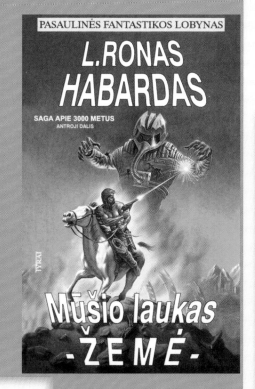

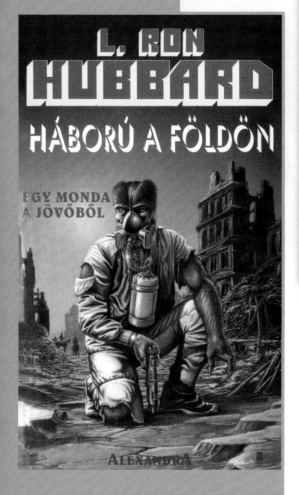

genre. Lauded across the critical spectrum as a feast of storytelling and "irresistible entertainment," as an "uplifting . . . saga of man's struggle and triumph," and by one reviewer, simply, as "Hubbard's back," *Battlefield Earth* swept across American bestseller lists for more than eight months in its original release. It then went on to become a milestone of contemporary fiction and one of the best-selling speculative fiction novels of all time. To date, nearly seven million copies of the novel have been sold in twenty-six languages in over fifty countries. Widely used as a study model in creative writing courses, *Battlefield Earth* was voted one of the top three of the hundred best English language novels of the last hundred years in a Modern Library Readers Poll. It has also garnered many other distinctions, among them the Saturn and Golden Scroll Awards in the United States, Italy's Tetradramma d'Oro critics' award for the novel's inherent message of peace and as a work of cultural significance, and the Gutenberg Award in France for its exceptional contribution to science fiction literature.

There is yet another literary quarter of particular consequence that has given the novel and its author its enthusiastic praise—L. Ron Hubbard's fellow science fiction writers, old and new, but especially those who, like Hubbard, were major contributors to the genre's golden age.

"I read *Battlefield Earth* straight through in one sitting although it's immense," Frederik Pohl said at the time. "I was fascinated by it." And then he added, definitively, "Ron Hubbard exploded onto the science fiction scene nearly half a century ago, and the reverberations haven't died yet."

For A.E. van Vogt, it was categorically "pure science fiction . . . written by a super-writer of the Golden Age of Science Fiction . . . a masterpiece."

L. Ron Hubbard wrote *Battlefield Earth* in 1980 while living in Newport Beach, California, less than a hundred miles from Encinitas, where nearly half a century earlier he had launched his legendary career in pulp fiction. Working at fresh creative peaks and with matchless productivity, he completed the massive *Battlefield Earth* manuscript along with some seven hundred pages of handwritten preliminary notes to the novel that are, themselves, a master's document on the rigors of literary craftsmanship. To that, in the same astounding period, he added the words and music to *Battlefield Earth,* destined to become the first-ever musical soundtrack for a novel, and wrote two full screenplays—a boisterous spy romp titled *Ai! Pedrito!* and an equally uproarious adventure in time, *A Very Strange Trip*—both of which would later become *New York Times* bestsellers in novelized form.

Then—and again we know the exact date from his copious notes—on December 22, 1980, L. Ron Hubbard embarked on a new literary project of unprecedented proportions—*Mission Earth*.

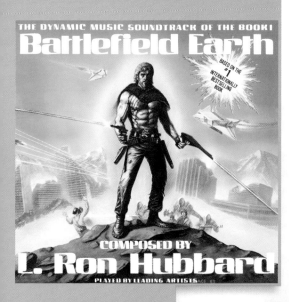

THE DYNAMIC MUSIC SOUNDTRACK OF THE BOOK!
Battlefield Earth
BASED ON THE #1 INTERNATIONALLY BEST SELLING BOOK
COMPOSED BY
L. Ron Hubbard
PLAYED BY LEADING ARTISTS

Battlefield Earth
Music soundtrack for the novel. Words and music by L. Ron Hubbard. Performed by Chick Corea, Gayle Moran Corea and Nicky Hopkins.

Death of a Tolnep   Artist: Joe Spencer
"The sheer force of it had knocked the Tolnep out. The faceplate was shattered; the strange eyes were glazed and rolled up into the head."

The Learning Machine   Artist: Corey Wolfe

"The monster now pointed to two windows on the front of the object. Then it pointed to a single lever that stuck out from the front of it. The monster pushed the lever down. Jonnie's eyes went round. He backed up. The object talked!"

Chrissie Dreams of Rescue   Artist: Jim Warren

"What does she look like? Black eyes and corn-silk hair. How was she formed? Beautiful and comely. How did she feel? Crushed with despair, hardly daring to hope for rescue."

Man, the Endangered Species   Artist: Frank Frazetta

"'Man,' said Terl, 'is an endangered species.'"

—opening line of *Battlefield Earth*

Vision   Artist: Shun Kijima
"If you will let me guide you, if you will each one contribute men and time to a daring enterprise... we will have a chance of everlasting victory!"

The Legend   Artist: Shun Kijima
"If you ask almost anyone on a civilized planet where he is, you are likely to be told that he is there, *just over that hill."*

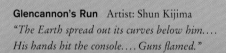

Glencannon's Run   Artist: Shun Kijima
"The Earth spread out its curves below him.... His hands hit the console.... Guns flamed."

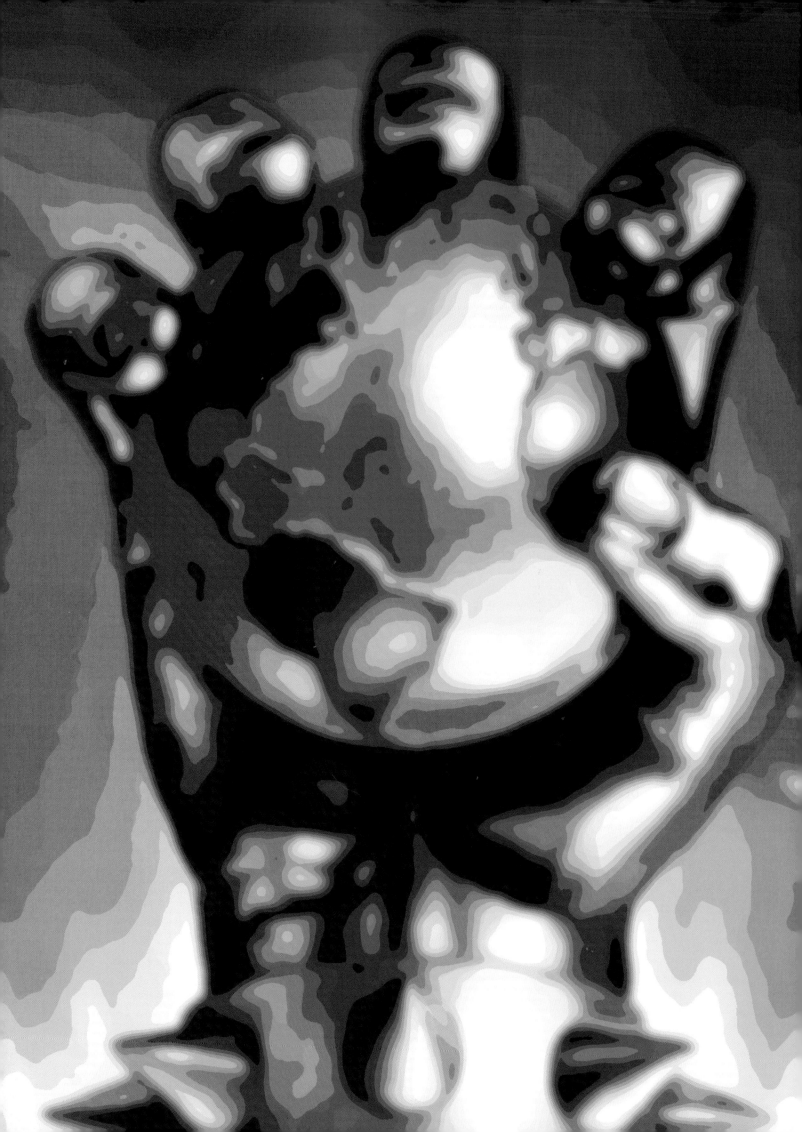

MISSION EARTH

"He breaks all the rules," said the *Everett (Washington) Herald,* getting to the very heart of L. Ron Hubbard's ten-volume magnum opus of intergalactic adventure and gale-force social satire, *Mission Earth.* "The old master has created a new genre and a veritable blockbuster," the newspaper went on, "and moves the art of science fiction into a new realm of entertainment as well as education."

Hubbard not only broke all the rules but he blazed a new literary path when he completed the monumental 1.2-million-word

Following **Battlefield Earth**, Ron completed his ten-volume magnum opus **Mission Earth** — between the two, a total of some 1.6 million words in just under twenty months.

The Invaders Plan Artist: Gerry Grace
"This particular target is known as Blito-P3 — the local inhabitants call it 'Earth.' It is a humanoid planet. . . . It lies on our invasion route into this galaxy and will be needed as a supply base."

Mission Earth in slightly less than eight months, on August 19, 1981. Like *Battlefield Earth* before it, *Mission Earth* was accompanied by voluminous handwritten notes that are a veritable guidebook to the creative process. What L. Ron Hubbard produced in those eight months, with inordinate speed, discipline and skill, was a remarkable interweaving of deftly plotted action, adventure, intrigue and espionage, all flavored with scathing social satire. "Jonathan Swift with a laser gun," as one critic put it, trained on the foibles and follies, the frayed institutions and the cultural sacred cows of contemporary civilization and the human condition.

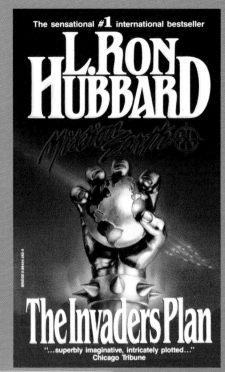

Cover art by Gerry Grace for *The Invaders Plan*, volume one in the *Mission Earth* series. All ten volumes were *New York Times* bestsellers.

Cover art by Gerry Grace for *Black Genesis* and *The Enemy Within*, volumes two and three in the *Mission Earth* series.

"You will lose sleep. You will miss appointments. If you don't force yourself to set it down and talk to your family from time to time, you may be looking for a new place to live. Reading **The Invaders Plan** is simply the most fun you can have by yourself.... Ironic, exciting, romantic and hilarious. It delighted me from the beginning. Remember how you felt the first time you saw Star Wars? This book will do it to you again."

—Orson Scott Card

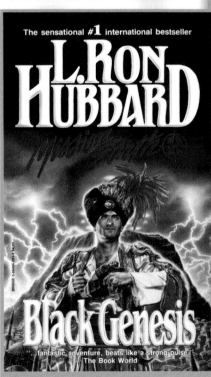

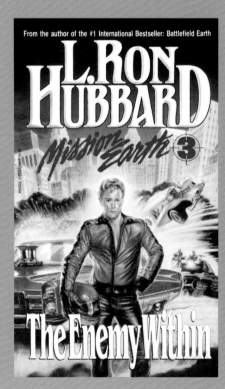

The Countess
Artist: Frank Frazetta
"With no change of expression whatever, she walked at a normal pace straight at that wild, freshly captured lepertige!"

Cover art by Gerry Grace for *An Alien Affair*, volume four in the *Mission Earth* series.

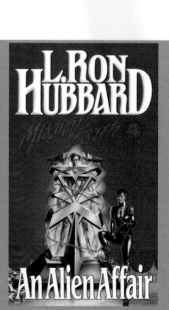

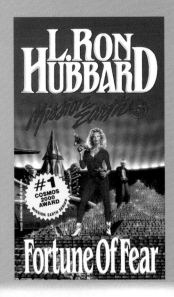

Cover art by Gerry Grace for *Fortune of Fear*, volume five in the *Mission Earth* series.

Universe-wide in its speculative reach, *Mission Earth* is the story of a secret invasion of Earth recounted by aliens from the planet Voltar, deep in the reaches of our own galaxy, who unrecognized and undetected already live and work among us. Prefaced by an official denial that "Blito-P3" (that's Earth in Voltarian cosmology) exists or has, in fact, ever existed, and based on a plaintively comic "confession" by disgraced secret operative Soltan Gris, the action of *Mission Earth* surges through immense stretches of the Galaxy and into mysterious, hidden places of Earth.

The Grand Council of the 110-planet Voltarian Confederation has targeted Earth for conquest so it may serve as a staging area for further Voltarian conquests across the Galaxy and beyond. But the Council has become convinced that it must send a mission to prevent Earth from rendering itself uninhabitable, and thus useless as a base, through its self-destructive pollution, nuclear contamination, drug abuse, lawlessness and other pandemic problems.

The "Mission Earth" of the book's title is assigned to Fleet Combat Engineer Jettero Heller, a heroically defined Hubbard protagonist whose loyalties, at first, make him ingenuously vulnerable. Charged with stemming Earth's deterioration without revealing his presence or improving the planet's ability to defend itself, Heller's mission is daunting enough. But it is complicated by the fact that he is unaware he is carrying audio and video implants which allow Soltan Gris to see and hear everything he does. Heller also has no idea that the treasonous head of Voltar's infamous Coordinated Information Apparatus, Lombar Hisst, wants his mission to fail as well. Heller's quest is orchestrated by Hubbard with adroit workmanship and pointed humor, leading one reviewer to call the story "a brilliantly conceived fusion of action, romance, satire and drama."

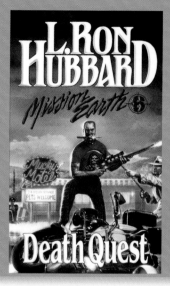

Death Quest is the sixth volume in the *Mission Earth* series. Cover art by Gerry Grace.

Intricately plotted and lucently imagined, *Mission Earth* unfolds in a procession of strange, unforgettable places, events and cultures, populated by everything from venal politicians, dangerously inept bureaucracies and the criminal underworld of two planets to alien races and some curiously talented domestic—and galactic—animal life. In the swirl of events, Heller meets the deliciously dangerous wild-animal trainer Countess Krak in the fortress prison of Spiteos. On Earth, he comes to grips with the devious stratagems of the powerful Delbert John Rockecenter. Hisst's conspiracy, meanwhile, deepens and darkens and the long, ominous shadows of future events begin to accumulate around the Voltar Confederation and its invisible Palace City. Effectively, Palace City is never really there, unassailably protected by a black hole that keeps the city thirteen minutes in the future. So, at least at first, it is safe.

In addition to the principals of the novel, there are other targets of what New York's *Newsday* called Hubbard's "satiric zingers," such as unappetizing public relations man J. Walter Madison, Voltar's Dr. Crobe and his infamous "cellological" experiments, and the celebrated thug Bang-Bang Rimbombo. There is also a roster of shady functionaries on Earth and Voltar with such whimsically evocative names as Bury, Raht, Terb, Bawtch and Ske. As one critic described this barbed wordplay: "[Hubbard] is good, really good, at pricking bubbles and blasting our assumptions, while providing us with action, humor and fun."

Mission Earth's fascinating diversity also includes Voltar's notorious Joy City; Manco—Heller and Countess Krak's home planet—and the colorful Manco Devil; *Tug One,* Heller's spacecraft, with its time-space-warp Will-be Was propulsion system; Krak's remarkable lepertiges, cat-like animals as tall as a man; and Mister Calico, a cat trained in the art of abduction.

Cover art by Gerry Grace for *Voyage of Vengeance*, volume seven in the *Mission Earth* series.

Jettero and Hightee Heller
Artist: Dave Willardson
"The eyes were languorous looking, the mouth was pursed in a huge kiss, the cheeks were blue, symbolizing longing. [The mask] made her look even prettier. Nothing could disguise the beauty of Hightee Heller."

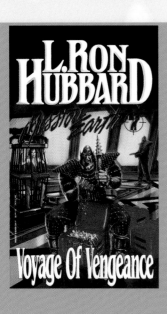

Parade of Acts   Artist: Ilene Meyers

"We were…watching the weekly 'freak parade.'… Lombar seemed to be quite agitated. He was fiddling with his stinger, probably to hide the shaking of his hands."

Cover art by Gerry Grace for *Disaster*, volume eight in the *Mission Earth* series.

Grand Council   Artist: Gary Meye

"The King's Own Astrographer tapped the top sheet of the report…. A startled shock had gone around the whole vast table."

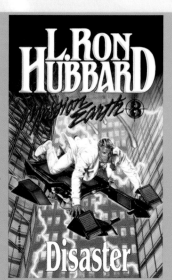

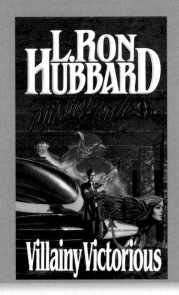

Beyond that, the futuristic technologies envisioned by L. Ron Hubbard in *Mission Earth* two decades ago—like the technical "heralds of possibility" in *Battlefield Earth*—offer some striking resonances in our time. The audio and video implants that make Jettero Heller a walking telecommunications center, for example, have distinct analogues in the information-monitoring microchip implants that have now begun to emerge as a twenty-first-century technology.

Comparably, with the detection of more than a hundred planets in the Milky Way Galaxy alone—including several with apparent "first cousin" similarities to our own solar system—the existence of a Voltar, perhaps even a planetary confederation, has become an increasingly arguable possibility. And, finally, the potential creation of an artificial black hole, optically or sonically, has been under exploration for some time by researchers at Sweden's Royal Institute of Technology, Austria's University of Innsbruck and elsewhere, lending intriguing new dimensions to the time-warping black hole Hubbard installed behind Voltar's Palace City.

The Invaders Plan, the first hardcover volume in the *Mission Earth* "dekalogy"—a word introduced by L. Ron Hubbard to describe the novel's unique ten-volume structure—was published in December 1985. That event began a publishing phenomenon without parallel then or since. In slightly less than two years—the final volume, *The Doomed Planet,* appeared in November 1987—all ten books in succession became *New York Times* and national, and then international, bestsellers. In fact, the series attained such popularity that, at one point, no fewer than seven volumes were on top-ten bestseller lists at the same time, prompting author and academician James Gunn to observe that "I don't know anything in publishing history to compare with it."

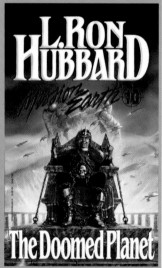

Cover art by Gerry Grace for
The Doomed Planet, volume ten
in the *Mission Earth* series.

The Countess Krak   Artist: Joe Spencer

*"Three hundred feet below us, in the space where the tug had been, there was a single guardsman,
isolated from the riot. . . . It was the Countess Krak! . . . She was very tiny now, far down there on Voltar.
She stopped throwing kisses and stood there sort of slumped."*

With an array of awards including France's prestigious Cosmos 2000 and Italy's Nova Science Fiction Award (Hubbard was the first non-Italian writer to receive it), the *Mission Earth* dekalogy has sold more than 7.7 million copies in thirteen languages—a publishing event, by any measure.

The magnitude of the work has been repeatedly underscored over the years by reviewers and critics like *Bookwatch*, for example, which singled it out as "one of the most impressive literary achievements in the science fiction genre"; or the Midwest Book Review, which hailed it as a work of "splendid talent combined with careful workmanship that is the very definition of conceptual quality—sought by so many and achieved by so few"; or the reviewer who said, so simply, that *Mission Earth* is "an L. Ron Hubbard masterpiece destined to become a classic."

As with *Battlefield Earth,* spirited approval has again come from other major speculative fiction writers. For fantasy's Anne McCaffrey, *Mission Earth* was and is "marvelous satire by a master of adventure." Author Gene Wolfe has lauded it as "wicked satire . . . more addictive than salt and peanuts." And science fiction author Orson Scott Card issued this warning: "You will lose sleep. You will miss appointments. If you don't force yourself to set it down and talk to your family from time to time, you may be looking for a new place to live."

Battlefield Earth and the *Mission Earth* series together dominated North American bestseller lists for 153 weeks. They became and remain today—along with *Fear, Final Blackout, Typewriter in the Sky* and so much more of L. Ron Hubbard's richly imaginative work—a memorable and vital part of the classic body of speculative fiction and of the popular literature of our time.

The Duelist and the Countess Krak
Artist: Dave Willardson
"I don't know what I expected to happen but it was not what happened. . . . a real live duelist leaped out. I felt the Countess instinctively go into combat posture. The thing looked vicious enough."

"I loved **Mission Earth**. *The CIA will hate it. Hubbard has produced a real knee-slapper . . . he's laughing at the Sacred Cow of the Eighties, the so-called intelligence community. . . . Few writers have had the knack of making a serious philosophical point without ever stopping to preach, without ever slowing the action for an instant."*
—Ray Faraday Nelson

"A big humorous tale of interstellar intrigue in the classical mold. I fully enjoyed it."
—Roger Zelazny

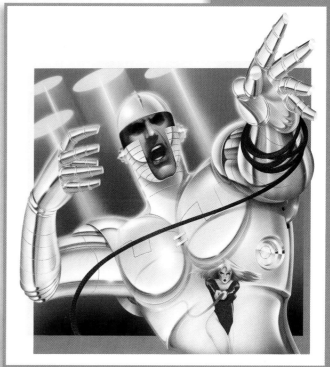

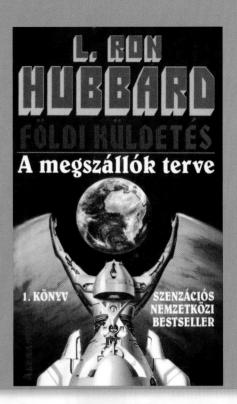

Russian, French and Hungarian editions.

Mission Earth HAS BEEN TRANSLATED INTO twelve languages: *Brazilian, Bulgarian, Chinese, Czech, French, German, Hungarian, Indonesian, Italian, Lithuanian, Portuguese and Russian.*

Chinese edition.

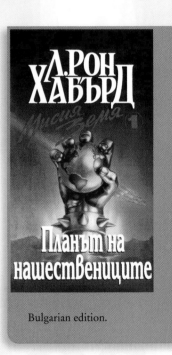

Bulgarian edition.

"*An incredibly good story, lushly written, vibrating with action and excitement. A gem.*"

— A.E. van Vogt

"**Mission Earth** *is a remarkable success story. I don't know anything in publishing history to compare with it.*"

— James Gunn, sf historian

"*Marvelous satire by a master of adventure.*"

— Anne McCaffrey

"*One of the most gripping storytellers in science fiction.*"

— Philip José Farmer

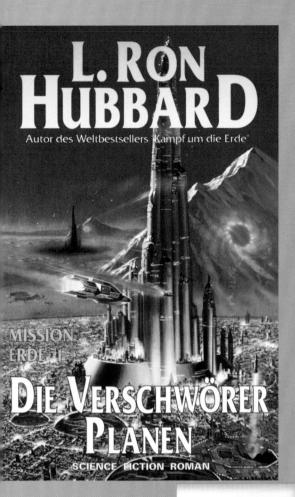

German edition.

Palace City   Artist: Gary Meyer

"Only a few miles away and a few thousand feet below lay Palace City.... The mountain behind it and the vast array of palaces are enwrapped in the effects of a gigantic space warp. The black hole in the mountain makes it invisible and this in turn causes Palace City to be invisible.... It is utterly impregnable."

Jettero Heller   Artist: Gary Meyer

"Jettero Heller was a combat engineer, an officer of the Royal Space Services.... Combat engineers [were] 'the daredevils of the Fleet.'"

Joy City   Artist: Gary Meyer

"The glittering lights and parks of Joy City spread out in a symphony of shapes and sparkles."

Tug One Artist: Greg Winters
*"'It has the engines of the biggest battleship in space.
It's the fastest thing in this universe!'... Tug One had just
become the mission ship for Mission Earth!"*

WORLDS OF TOMORROW

L Ron Hubbard was a singularly unselfish writer.

In the mid-1930s, soon after his own stories started appearing in the pages of America's popular fiction magazines, he shared his hard-earned experience with creative writing students in speaking engagements at institutions such as Harvard and George Washington University. In such forums, he offered practical advice on how to break into the ranks of professional writers.

When, in 1935, he was named president of the New York Chapter of the American Fiction Guild, he made it easier for writers to join the Guild and readily shared his knowledge of writing and publishing with others who sought his help.

Hubbard also generated a series of "how to" articles that appeared in a number of writing magazines in the 1930s and 1940s, offering guidance to help new writers navigate the obstacles they were likely to encounter. In 1940, as a feature of a radio program he hosted in Ketchikan, Alaska, while on an Explorers Club–sanctioned expedition, he offered advice for beginning writers and went one step further, initiating the "Golden Pen Award" contest to encourage listeners of station KGBU to write fiction, and he awarded prizes for the best stories submitted.

Years later, in recognition of the increasingly difficult path encountered between first manuscript and published work, particularly in an era in which publishers devote the lion's share of their promotional budgets to a few household names, L. Ron Hubbard "initiated a means for new and budding writers to have a chance for their creative efforts to be seen and acknowledged." He created the Writers of the Future Contest and, two decades later, the results of his prestigious contest speak for themselves.

As a seasoned professional by 1935, Hubbard was regularly called upon to pass along tips for novice writers in journals like this.

The Best of Writers of the Future, published in 2000. Cover art by Frank Frazetta.

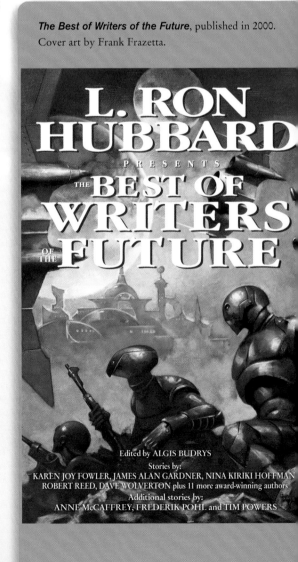

From the very outset of his long professional career, Hubbard gave generously of his time, energies and skills to help other writers—especially the beginner— become more able and productive at their craft.

Writers of the Future, Volume I.

Established in 1983, expressly for the aspiring writer, Writers of the Future has become the most respected and significant forum for new talent in all aspects of speculative fiction—science fiction, fantasy and horror. The elite character of the contest is evident from the roster of judges: Kevin J. Anderson, Doug Beason, Gregory Benford, Terry Brooks, Algis Budrys, Orson Scott Card, Hal Clement, Brian Herbert, Nina Kiriki Hoffman, Eric Kotani, Anne McCaffrey, Larry Niven, Andre Norton, Frederik Pohl, Jerry Pournelle, Tim Powers, Robert Silverberg and K. D. Wentworth. Over the years, other such luminaries as Ben Bova, Ramsey Campbell, Frank Herbert, Charles Sheffield, John Varley, Gene Wolfe, Roger Zelazny and three colleagues of Hubbard's from the fabled golden age— Jack Williamson, C. L. Moore and Theodore Sturgeon—have also all served as contest judges.

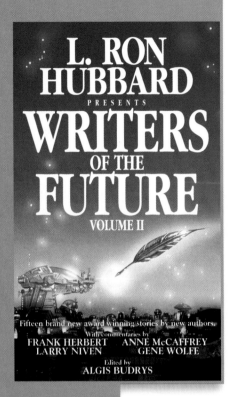

Writers of the Future, Volume II.

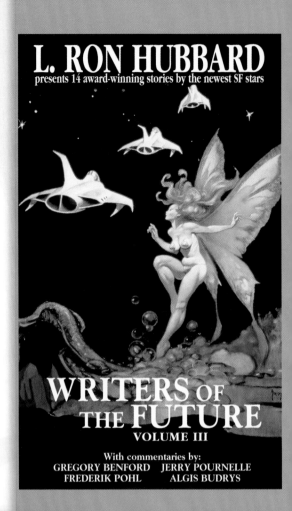

Writers of the Future, Volume III. Cover art by Frank Frazetta.

Writers of the Future, Volume IV.
Cover art by Frank Frazetta.

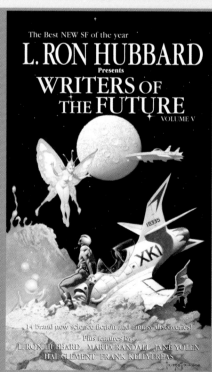

Writers of the Future, Volume V.
Cover art by Frank Frazetta.

"I know of no one who has done more for new writers of fantastic literature in the last decade than the Writers of the Future Contest. It is a credit to American literature and a singular, generous event."

—Dr. Gregory Benford

Writers of the Future, Volume VI.
Cover art by Frank Frazetta.

Writers of the Future, Volume VIII
Cover art by Gary Meyer.

Writers of the Future, Volume VII.
Cover art by Frank Frazetta.

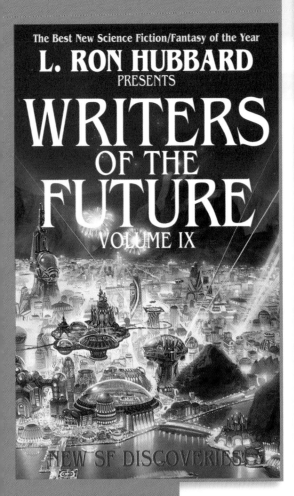

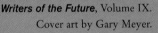

Writers of the Future, Volume IX.
Cover art by Gary Meyer.

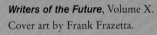

Writers of the Future, Volume X.
Cover art by Frank Frazetta.

In addition to cash awards, winning entries are published annually in the *L. Ron Hubbard Presents Writers of the Future* anthology, the first of which was released in 1985. The exciting offerings of the field's next generation are interspersed with insightful commentaries for new writers by the established professionals. By 2002, seventeen more anthologies had been published since that first one, with more on their way. As Algis Budrys notes, "Prepublication orders throughout the U.S. set records, and a succession of print order increases occurred at a gratifying and startling pace." Beyond that, the Writers of the Future anthologies have been used as instructional texts in creative writing and literature classes in scores of colleges and universities, including, among others, Rutgers University, Pepperdine University, the University of Kansas, the University of Houston and Brigham Young University.

The annual contest inspires both the writers of speculative literature and those who share that inspiration. The Writers of the Future annual awards ceremonies enjoy the support and participation of many of the world's most celebrated scientific figures. Nobel Prize–winning physicist Dr. Sheldon Glashow, for example, served as a panelist for award ceremonies held at the United Nations, while

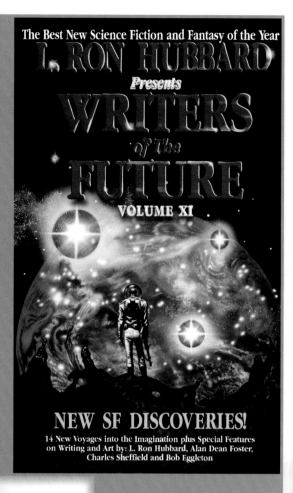

The Best New Science Fiction and Fantasy of the Year

L. RON HUBBARD
Presents
WRITERS
of The
FUTURE
VOLUME XI

NEW SF DISCOVERIES!

14 New Voyages into the Imagination plus Special Features on Writing and Art by: L. Ron Hubbard, Alan Dean Foster, Charles Sheffield and Bob Eggleton

Writers of the Future, Volume XI.
Cover art by Frank Kelly Freas.

The Best New Science Fiction and Fantasy of the Year

L. RON HUBBARD
Presents
WRITERS
of The
FUTURE
VOLUME XII

NEW SF DISCOVERIES

16 Voyages into the Imagination plus Special Features on Writing and Art by: L. Ron Hubbard, Doug Beason and Paul Lehr

Writers of the Future, Volume XII. Cover art by Bob Eggleton.

"*The contest has opened the way for scores of writers and has set them out on the fine careers they deserve.*"

—Jack Williamson

astronaut Story Musgrave (of Hubble Telescope repair fame) served in the same capacity for ceremonies at NASA's Space Center in Houston, Texas.

The Writers of the Future awards ceremony was the first such symposium held in the United Nations Trusteeship Council Chamber, and thus was the first celebration of speculative fiction on an official international stage. Hosting the event was Hans W. Janitschek, president of the United Nations Society of Writers and Artists, who remarked that "L. Ron Hubbard was a creator of the first order, blessed with an imagination beyond description. He saw and wrote the future, inspiring millions and awakening the genius of writing in thousands."

The prestige and influence of the Writers of the Future Contest led directly to the creation of its immensely popular adjunct, the Writing Workshop. Inaugurated in 1985, and affording contest winners personal critiques and instruction by such masters of the craft as Algis Budrys and Tim Powers, the Writing Workshop is an extension of magazine articles Hubbard authored in his early years for *Writer's Digest, Writer's Review,* the *Author & Journalist* and *Writers' Markets & Methods* to help other writers develop their talents. These articles, used today to teach the basic skills of story writing, combine compassion with encouragement for the fledgling writer, and continue to offer insightful lessons in writing techniques.

Writers of the Future, Volume XIII. Cover art by Frank Frazetta.

The Best New Science Fiction and Fantasy of the Year

L. RON HUBBARD
PRESENTS
WRITERS OF THE
FUTURE

VOLUME XIV

NEW SF DISCOVERIES
17 Tales of Creativity plus Special
Features by L. Ron Hubbard, Anne
McCaffrey and Vincent Di Fate.

Writers of the Future, Volume XIV. Cover art by Paul Lehr.

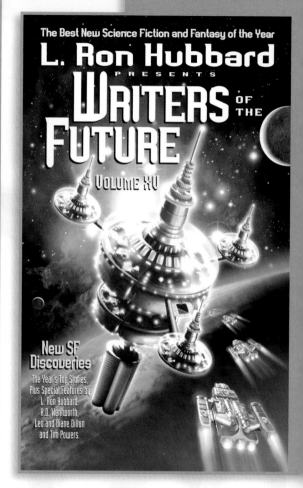

Writers of the Future, Volume XV.
Cover design by Peter Green.

The Best New Science Fiction and Fantasy of the Year

L. Ron Hubbard
PRESENTS
WRITERS OF THE
FUTURE

VOLUME XV

New SF
Discoveries
The Year's Top Stories,
Plus Special Features by
L. Ron Hubbard,
K.D. Wentworth,
Leo and Diane Dillon
and Tim Powers.

In 1988, Hubbard's vision inspired a companion contest for new and aspiring illustrators seeking to become speculative fiction artists. Winning illustrators—three each quarter—are assigned the winning stories from the writers' contest and illustrate them for the annual anthology. The list of judges for the illustrators' contest is no less impressive than that of the writers' contest and represents a virtual who's who of the field. Edd Cartier, Vincent Di Fate, Leo and Diane Dillon,

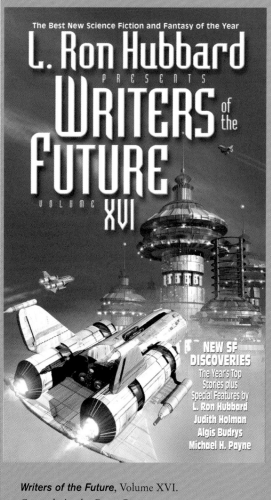

Writers of the Future, Volume XVI.
Cover design by Peter Green.

Writers of the Future, Volume XVII. Cover art by Frank Kelly Freas.

"What Hugo Gernsback did in the 1920s and 1930s and John W. Campbell, Jr., did through the 1940s and 1950s, the L. Ron Hubbard Writers of the Future Contest is doing in the 1980s and 1990s: identifying the writers who will shape the field into the next millennium."

—David Phalen
Writers of the Future 1992 Award Winner

Writers of the Future, Volume XVIII.
Cover art by Frank Frazetta.

Frank Frazetta, judge for the Illustrators of the Future Contest.

Frank Kelly Freas, Roger Zelazny
and Anne McCaffrey.

Judges K. D. Wentworth and Tim
Powers presenting writer winner
Jae Brim (center) with her award.

Algis Budrys instructs the L. Ron Hubbard Writing
Workshop at The George Washington University.

Bob Eggleton, Will Eisner, Frank Frazetta, Frank Kelly Freas, Laura Brodian Freas, Judith Holman, Shun Kijima, Jack Kirby, Paul Lehr, Ron Lindahn, Val Lakey Lindahn, Moebius, Sergey V. Poyarkov, Alex Schomburg, H. R. Van Dongen and William R. Warren, Jr., have all served as contest judges.

Just as L. Ron Hubbard intended, the Writers of the Future program has given novice writers an unparalleled opportunity to develop and market their creative efforts. The success of the program, however, cannot be defined simply by the number of deserving writers discovered through the merit competition or the number of students who have completed the Writing Workshop, or even by the number of writers who have been published in the annual anthology, many for the first time. The definitive measure of its success is its fulfillment of his legacy—that new writers are assured the opportunity and means to contribute to the literature and creative standards of today and tomorrow.

Since its inception, the contest has helped place more than two hundred and fifty new novels and close to twenty-five hundred short stories on American bookshelves. Furthermore, it has launched the professional careers of two hundred young authors, and has rightfully earned its accolade as "a credit to American literature and a singular, generous event." The Writers of the Future Award has also earned its place alongside the Hugo and Nebula Awards in the triad of speculative fiction's most prestigious acknowledgments of literary excellence. Just as L. Ron Hubbard, the writer, changed the genre in the twentieth century, so, too, is his legacy accomplishing the same feat as the twenty-first century blossoms.

"*A culture is as rich and as capable of surviving as it has imaginative artists. The artist is looked upon to start things. The artist injects the spirit of life into a culture. And through his creative endeavors, the writer works continually to give tomorrow a new form.*

"*In these modern times, there are many communication lines for works of art. Because a few works of art can be shown so easily to so many, there may even be fewer artists. The competition is very keen and even dagger sharp.*

"*It is with this in mind that I initiated a means for new and budding writers to have a chance for their creative efforts to be seen and acknowledged.*"

—L. Ron Hubbard
Introduction
Writers of the Future, Volume I

Pictured above, illustrator Frank Kelly Freas and science fiction authors Ramsey Campbell, Larry Niven and Frederik Pohl at a panel discussion on Writers of the Future.

The 2000, 1999 and 1990 Illustrators of the Future Grand Prize winners. From left to right: Andy B. Clarkson, Frank Wu and Sergey V. Poyarkov.

Ray Bradbury and Jack Williamson at the 10th Anniversary celebration of the Writers of the Future Contest.

An elated Karawynn Long with her trophy at the 1993 event.

Jack Williamson receives the L. Ron Hubbard Lifetime Achievement Award from Algis Budrys at the 1998 Writers of the Future annual awards ceremony.

The L. Ron Hubbard Gallery, located on Hollywood Boulevard in Hollywood, site of several of the Writers and Illustrators of the Future annual awards ceremonies.

JUDGES OF THE FUTURE

JUDGES FOR THE WRITERS OF THE FUTURE CONTEST

Kevin J. Anderson

Doug Beason

Gregory Benford

Ben Bova

Terry Brooks

Algis Budrys

Ramsey Campbell

Orson Scott Card

Hal Clement

Brian Herbert

Frank Herbert

Nina Kiriki Hoffman

Eric Kotani

Anne McCaffrey

C. L. Moore

Larry Niven

Andre Norton

Frederik Pohl

Jerry Pournelle

Tim Powers

Charles Sheffield

Robert Silverberg

Theodore Sturgeon

John Varley

K. D. Wentworth

Jack Williamson

Gene Wolfe

Roger Zelazny

JUDGES FOR THE ILLUSTRATORS OF THE FUTURE CONTEST

Edd Cartier

Vincent Di Fate

Diane Dillon

Leo Dillon

Bob Eggleton

Will Eisner

Frank Frazetta

Frank Kelly Freas

Laura Brodian Freas

Judith Holman

Shun Kijima

Jack Kirby

Paul Lehr

Ron Lindahn

Val Lakey Lindahn

Moebius

Sergey V. Poyarkov

Alex Schomburg

H. R. Van Dongen

William R. Warren, Jr.

L. RON HUBBARD

A BIOGRAPHICAL CHRONOLOGY

Capturing my own dreams in words, paint or music and then seeing them live is the highest kind of excitement," L. Ron Hubbard wrote early in his remarkably diverse and prolific career. It was, as well, an excitement he drew with consummate skill from a life of adventurous breadth and uncommon personal achievement—as an explorer and ethnologist, master mariner and daredevil pilot, filmmaker and photographer, philosopher and educator, composer and musician, and, always, before everything, as a writer and master storyteller. His boundless curiosity, his deep conviction that "To really know life you've got to be part of life. You must get down and look; you must get into the nooks and crannies of existence," carried him across continents and oceans and through the wide realm of the human condition. And all of it, first to last, became part both of L. Ron Hubbard's fiction and of the literary culture of our time. The biographical chronology that follows profiles, although it cannot fully encompass, the dimensions of his life and work.

EARLY YEARS 1911–1926

1911 Lafayette Ronald Hubbard is born in Tilden, Nebraska, on March 13, to U.S. naval officer Harry Ross Hubbard and Ledora May Waterbury. In September, they move to Durant, Oklahoma.

The Hubbard family lives briefly in the city of Kalispell, Montana. An early bond of friendship is formed in the fall of 1913 as young Ron dances to the beat of Indian drums and impresses Blackfeet Indians at a tribal ceremony held on the outskirts of town.

From there, the Hubbards move to just outside of Helena, Montana, where the family ranch, affectionately referred to as the "Old Homestead," becomes their home. In the harsh frontier winter months, they retreat to a three-story brick house on the corner of Fifth and Beatty in Helena. Here, in the "Big Sky" country

Ron with his mother, Ledora May; his grandfather's feed and granary can be seen in the background.

Helena, Montana, circa 1914: an early portrait Ron's parents entitled "The Old Scout."

U.S. Navy Commander Joseph "Snake" Thompson.

Circa 1920: Fishing with his father, Harry Ross Hubbard, while en route to Oakland, California, from Helena.

Seattle, Washington, 1923: Ron would become the nation's youngest Eagle Scout the following year, at the age of 13.

of pioneer Montana, young Ron learns to read and write at an early age, rides horses and breaks broncos, pans for gold, and is honored with the status of Blood Brother of the Blackfeet Indians by age six.

1918 Ron and his grandfather embark on a springtime "automotive adventure" in a Model T Ford, driving from Helena to Portland, Oregon. He returns to Helena and, from there, adventures on his own by train to Tacoma, Washington. In 1919, he moves with his parents to San Diego and a year later to Oakland, California.

1923 The Hubbard family moves to Tacoma and Ron joins local Boy Scout Troop 31 in April. In October, his father is ordered to report to Washington, D.C. The Hubbard family boards the USS *Ulysses S. Grant* on November 1, sailing from San Francisco to New York through the newly reopened Panama Canal. During this voyage, Hubbard meets U.S. Navy Commander Joseph "Snake" Thompson, recently returned from studies in Vienna with Sigmund Freud. In the course of the friendship that follows in Washington, D.C., Commander Thompson introduces him further to Freud's theories and encourages him to conduct his own investigations into the nature of the mind.

1924 Now an active member of Washington, D.C.'s Boy Scout Troop 10, Ron earns numerous merit badges, Life Scout and Star Scout medals, and on March 20, he represents his troop and meets President Calvin Coolidge. Five days later, on March 25, he becomes the nation's youngest Eagle Scout. The following day he returns to Montana by cross-country train.

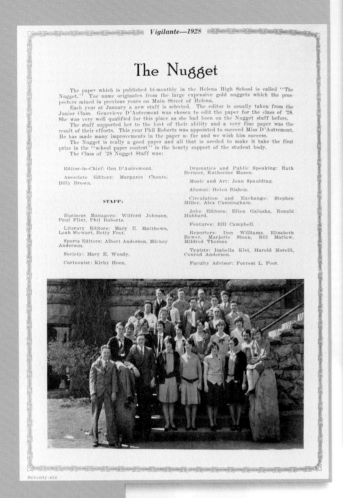

Helena High School, 1927, where Ron becomes an editor of the school's newspaper, the *Nugget*.

At the dawn of a writing career: Ron as a staff writer on the Helena High School *Nugget* stands second row from top, center.

YOUTHFUL ADVENTURES 1927–1933

1927 During early June, Ron travels to San Francisco and embarks on a voyage to Guam via Hawaii, Japan, China, Hong Kong and the Philippines. In the first week of July he meets his father in Guam. During these travels, he carefully records his adventures and observations. Articles about his journeys appear in the Helena High School *Nugget* and the *Helena Independent*.

By September, he is back in Helena and becomes an editor of the Helena High School *Nugget*. In October, he joins the Montana National Guard's 163rd Infantry.

1928 In early May, as the school year is drawing to a close, he organizes and enters a group of classmates in Helena's annual Vigilante Day Parade. They receive the "Most Original" award for his entry of Spanish Main pirates. This and other events are carefully recorded in a ledger along with short stories based on his travels. He will continue recording fragments of stories in that ledger for the next two years.

Hubbard leaves Helena again in May, and in July travels aboard the USS *Henderson* from San Diego to Guam. From there, during the next fourteen months, he journeys inland to the western hills of China, back to Japan, down to the Philippines, and south to Java. He befriends a British intelligence officer, Buddhist priests, a man who is last in a line of magicians descending from the court of Kublai

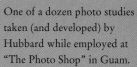
One of a dozen photo studies taken (and developed) by Hubbard while employed at "The Photo Shop" in Guam.

Guam, 1928, during a fourteen-month journey that takes Ron to China and the Forbidden City, Japan, the Philippines, and south to Java.

Guam, 1928: a photograph taken by Hubbard of indigenous caribou ridden by natives in shallow water.

Beijing (Peking), 1928: Hubbard and his parents at the Forbidden City.

The Great Wall of China, near Nan-Kou Pass, west of Beijing, photographed by L. Ron Hubbard.

Khan, and meets people from many varied cultures and backgrounds. Hubbard gains greater nautical expertise aboard the twin-masted coastal schooner *Marianna Maru* as he plies the waters off the China coast as a helmsman and supercargo. A selection of his photographs from these travels is purchased by the stock photograph house Underwood and Underwood, and by *National Geographic*.

1929   Hubbard returns to the United States in September to complete his high-school education. He attends Swavely Prep School in Manassas, Virginia, where he writes a number of school papers, including "Should the Philippines Be Liberated?" "Modernism," "Go Thou Fair Lad and Discover Thy Imagination," and a book report on *Revolt in the Desert* by T. E. Lawrence, more familiarly known as Lawrence of Arabia.

1930   In February, Hubbard enrolls at Woodward School for Boys in Washington, D.C. In March, he writes and delivers a prize-winning speech on "The Constitution—A Guarantee of Liberty to the Individual" in a regional oratory contest.

He enlists in the 20th Marine Corps Reserve, Company G, during May, is appointed first sergeant in June, and turns out a prize-winning drill team.

Hubbard graduates from Woodward and in September enrolls at George Washington University (GWU). His studies include engineering courses and atomic and molecular phenomena, but here he also carries out his first investigation of the structure and function of the human mind. Earlier, during the summer, he launches a professional writing career, scripting dramas for radio station WJSV while attending classes at George Washington University. He also writes and performs ballads on local station WOL, all the while employed as a photojournalist/reporter by the *Washington Herald*.

1931   While Hubbard continues his studies at GWU, he takes up glider flying, becomes recognized as a daring pilot, and sets a national soaring record for sustained flight over the same field. He also becomes a powered-flight pilot and barnstorms across the Midwest in September with a friend. He is elected president of The George Washington University Flying Club, is secretary of the GWU chapter of the American Society of Civil Engineers, and joins a team of surveyors sent to verify the U.S.-Canadian border in Maine.

1932   In January, Hubbard sells his first magazine article, "Tailwind Willies," to the aviation journal *Sportsman Pilot*. In it, he details the latest aviation developments and advises pilots on flight procedures in adverse conditions.

As an editor and writer for the *University Hatchet* at GWU, Hubbard produces his first published fiction story, "Tah," in February, and a short adventure story, "Grounded," in April. Both are peripherally based on personal experiences or the experiences of people he encountered in the Far East. In May, Hubbard wins the Literary Award at GWU for the best one-act play with "The God Smiles," drawn from his travels in China.

In the spring, Hubbard organizes and leads the Caribbean Motion Picture Expedition. He is joined on the two-and-a-half-month, five-thousand-mile journey aboard the two-hundred-foot, four-masted schooner *Doris Hamlin* by more

The George Washington University, where Hubbard's first published fiction story, **"Tah,"** appears in the school's literary magazine in February 1932, followed by an award-winning one-act play.

The two-hundred-foot *Doris Hamlin,* one of the last of the full four-masted schooners, used by Hubbard for his five-thousand-mile 1932 Caribbean Motion Picture Expedition.

The first sluice of the West Indies Mineralogical Expedition near San Juan, Puerto Rico, November 1932.

L. Ron Hubbard (far left) with three pioneering aerial colleagues at the Washington, D.C., airport, 1932.

than fifty adventure-seeking college students. The voyage is completed by September. The crew brings numerous floral and reptile specimens back for the University of Michigan and Ron's photographs are sold to the *New York Times*.

In October, he embarks upon a voyage to Puerto Rico. As part of the West Indies Mineralogical Expedition, he not only completes the first mineralogical survey of Puerto Rico as an American territory but writes articles for the *Sportsman Pilot* about flying through the Caribbean Islands. He also investigates and explores some of the area's diverse cultures and beliefs, including voodoo and Espiritismo.

In November, his "Sans Power" appears in the *Sportsman Pilot*. His first nautical story, "Submarine," appears in the *University Hatchet* the same month.

1933 The expedition to Puerto Rico is completed in April. In May, Hubbard's article "Washington's Langley Day" appears in the *Sportsman Pilot*.

Hubbard returns to the mainland and soon moves to a small California beachfront town north of San Diego. There, while continuing to do articles for the *Sportsman Pilot,* he also begins his professional career as a writer of fiction. With customary gusto, each day he writes a story ranging in length from 4,500 to 20,000 words and submits it to New York publishers in an attempt to crack the market. It takes him six weeks and then he sells two stories for three hundred dollars—a princely sum in days when hamburger costs ten cents a pound. By the end of the year he is writing at a more relaxed pace—what will become his average 100,000 words a month.

THE LEGEND BEGINS 1934–1937

1934   "The Green God," Hubbard's first fiction story to be published in a popular fiction magazine, appears in *Thrilling Adventures* in February. By December, after placing numerous stories, he hires an agent to represent his work. Employing a variety of pen names, he publishes an average of more than one story every two weeks—adding up to some 138 novels, novelettes and short stories in a six-year period. The stories cover a wide spectrum of genres, including adventure, western, mystery and detective.

1935   The New York Chapter of the American Fiction Guild elects him president, and Hubbard lends his leadership skills to a group that includes Raymond Chandler, Dashiell Hammett and Edgar Rice Burroughs. His articles about writing appear in the

San Diego, California, circa 1934.
"I wrote to the best of my ability and with great sincerity."

Hollywood, California, circa 1935. The writers' complex at Columbia Studios where Hubbard scripts **The Secret of Treasure Island**.

Author & Journalist and *Writer's Review* and he guests on radio shows to discuss ways aspiring writers can improve the quality and salability of their stories.

1936 Hubbard completes his first hardcover novel, *Buckskin Brigades,* in November. It is published in July 1937 by the Macaulay Company. The work is drawn, in part, from his youthful experiences with Montana's Blackfeet tribesmen.

1937 Columbia Pictures purchases film rights to his novel *Murder at Pirate Castle* and asks him to write the screenplay adaptation, which is produced under the title *The Secret of Treasure Island.* He works on other big-screen serials for Columbia—*The Adventures of the Mysterious Pilot* and *The Great Adventures of Wild Bill Hickok.* He also collaborates on *The Spider* series with Norvell Page at Columbia Pictures. During his ten weeks in Hollywood, he writes a quarter of a million words for scripts and continues to produce stories for his New York editors.

Changing Genres 1938–1941

1938 Hubbard returns to New York where executives from Street & Smith, one of the world's largest publishers, enlist his help to fill the pages of their newly retitled magazine *Astounding Science Fiction.* He is asked to boost sagging sales with stories about *real* people—not robots and machines. He continues to write in other genres, but his decision to enter the field of science fiction is one which fundamentally changes the genre. "The Dangerous Dimension," his first story for *Astounding Science Fiction,* appears in the July issue.

1939 In January, John W. Campbell, Jr., editor of *Astounding Science Fiction,* starts *Unknown* magazine to provide a venue for "fantasy" stories, particularly those that Hubbard writes. Hubbard's first story for *Unknown,* "The Ultimate Adventure," appears in the April issue.

1940 The Explorers Club elects him a member in February. *Death's Deputy* is published the same month. *Final Blackout* is published in three parts between April and June. In June, the same month that *Fear* is published in *Unknown,* Hubbard sets sail from Seattle under Explorers Club flag number 105, in the thirty-two-foot ketch *Magician,* on the Alaskan Radio Experimental Expedition. He charts previously unrecorded hazards and coastline for the U.S. Navy Hydrographic Office, conducts experiments on radio directional finding, and examines local native cultures. He also does a series of radio shows on KGBU in Ketchikan, Alaska. Then, in December, he announces a Christmas story writing contest for Alaska's amateur writers in the "Golden Pen Award" hour.

Puget Sound, Washington, spring 1940. L. Ron Hubbard conducts test trials for the thirty-two-foot ketch *Magician*, soon to embark on the Alaskan Radio Experimental Expedition, under flag #105 of the Explorers Club.

Hubbard in Ketchikan, Alaska, November 1940, having charted uncertain coastal waters for the U.S. Navy and field-tested an experimental navigational system.

Broadcasting a series of radio shows on Ketchikan's KGBU, Hubbard launches a "Golden Pen Award" contest for Alaska's amateur writers, December 1940.

"The Kilkenny Cats" is published in September and *Typewriter in the Sky* is published in two parts in November and December.

The U.S. Bureau of Marine Inspection and Navigation awards him the "Master of Steam and Motor Vessels" license in December. After he is back home in the Seattle area, he presents the U.S. Navy with hundreds of photographs and notes from his expedition and resumes his writing.

1941   Hubbard receives the "Master of Sail Vessels" license for "Any Ocean" in late March. The United States Navy commissions him as lieutenant (jg) in the Navy Reserve in late June. With the outbreak of war on December 7, he is ordered to active duty. He reports to Australia where he coordinates naval intelligence activities as Senior Officer Present Ashore. Nine stories, written earlier, are published between January 1942 and April 1943.

Elected to the Explorers Club in February 1940, L. Ron Hubbard conducts three major sea-and-land expeditions under the Club's storied pennant between 1940 and 1966.

New York City headquarters of the renowned Explorers Club, whose members have included Sir Edmund Hillary, Admiral Richard E. Byrd and Robert Peary.

Hubbard in 1943 when he captains the Navy subchaser PC 815.

The Explorers Journal

Vol. XXVIII   WINTER-SPRING, 1950   No. 1

One of L. Ron Hubbard's first published articles on his breakthrough explorations into the human mind is published under the title "**Terra Incognita: The Mind**" in the Winter–Spring 1950 issue of the Explorers Club journal.

WAR YEARS 1942–1945

Hubbard returns to the United States from Australia and in the summer assumes command of convoy escort YP 422 in Boston. He attends submarine chaser school in Miami and commands the subchaser PC 815 in the North Pacific, where he engages enemy submarines in two separate encounters off the coast of Oregon. He also instructs at the Small Craft Training Center in San Pedro, California, is a navigation officer aboard the USS *Algol,* and attends the U.S. Navy School of Military Government at Princeton University. As the war enters its final months, he is sent to Oak Knoll Naval Hospital in Oakland, California, to receive care for injuries sustained during the war.

At Oak Knoll, Hubbard conducts a series of experiments dealing with the endocrine system and discovers that, contrary to long-standing beliefs, function monitors structure in the relationship between thought and the body. He begins to help fellow veterans "who had not survived the war too well."

POSTWAR FICTION 1946–1949

1946   Released from active duty in February, Hubbard returns to fiction writing as a means of supporting his intensified research.

1947-1949   By July, "The Chee-Chalker" is published. In the next three years (up to November 1950), he publishes forty-seven science fiction, fantasy, western, mystery and detective stories. Among these are "Blood on His Spurs," "Ole Doc Methuselah," "Killer's Law," *To the Stars, The Kingslayer, The Masters of Sleep,* "Hoss Tamer" and "The Obsolete Weapon." During these years, he serves as a special officer with the Los Angeles Police Department and conducts Dianetics research in cities across the United States, including Los Angeles, Savannah, New York City and Washington, D.C. He also writes the original thesis of Dianetics, which is circulated widely among doctors, engineers and scientists across the country, and publishes his first articles on the subject, "Terra Incognita: The Mind" (*Explorers Journal,* Winter–Spring 1950) and "Dianetics: The Evolution of a Science" (*Astounding Science Fiction,* May 1950).

EXPLORING TERRA INCOGNITA 1950–1979

1950   In May, Hermitage House publishes *Dianetics: The Modern Science of Mental Health,* which culminates Hubbard's years of research on the subject of the mind. The public response is telling: a *New York Times* bestseller that remains on the list for twenty-six consecutive weeks, sweeping public interest, and demand for more information and lectures. Hubbard leaves the field of fiction and Hollywood movie offers to devote his time to these demands. By 1952, his research leads him to develop Scientology applied religious philosophy. For the next three decades, he dedicates his life to writing and publishing millions of words of nonfiction concerning the nature of man and the betterment of the human condition.

   During this time, he also writes, lectures and researches extensively in fields ranging from drug rehabilitation and organizational management to art and communications, while he advances and refines his understanding of the human mind and spirit. He still finds time for some notable achievements in exploration and writing.

1960   Hubbard rescripts the German film classic *Blue Light* for Britain's Adventure Films Production and drafts a cinematic treatment for an educational film aimed at Bantu tribesmen in South Africa.

1961   Hubbard receives his second Explorers Club flag for the "Ocean Archeological Expedition to study underwater sites of historical interest such as submerged cities" in the Aegean Sea. He enrolls in the famous New York Institute of

Photography's correspondence course to familiarize himself with photographic advancements. Thereafter, he is periodically engrossed in a number of photographic projects: "East Grinstead—A Photo Story," "A Student Comes to Saint Hill" and "Sir Robert Fosset's Circus."

1964   His circus and English landscape photographs are selected for salon showings in Belgium and the International Photographic Exhibition in Nantes, France.

1965   While on a "photographic holiday" in Spain, he obtains permission from Las Palmas officials to photograph the bullfights. Equipped with telephoto lens and a Voigtlander, he completes a memorable series. Also from these travels come Canary Island landscapes and portraits of flamenco dancers.

1966   He accepts his third Explorers Club flag for the Hubbard Geological Survey Expedition, which amplifies existing knowledge of Mediterranean history.

Hubbard at the Sir Robert Fosset Circus, 1964.

Hubbard's photographs of Sir Robert Fosset's country circus are selected for showing at the 1964 International Photographic Exhibition in Nantes, France.

1973 Hubbard organizes a complex shoot of the Lisbon Maritime Museum, including an ingenious series of photos of the Vasco da Gama flagship in miniature in Lisbon harbor. Also from this Lisbon stay are his official portraits of Portuguese Prime Minister Marcello Caetano.

1975 Hubbard continues his photographic work, including a project on behalf of the Curaçao Tourist Board, with a special series of architectural shots of the island's historic synagogues.

1977 He completes the script for a feature-length science fiction epic, *Revolt in the Stars*.

Self-portrait taken in 1972.

Hubbard uses a scale model of Vasco da Gama's flagship in miniature to capture this ingenious photograph in Lisbon's harbor, 1973.

MONUMENTAL RETURN TO FICTION 1980–1981

During 1980–1981, Hubbard produces two million words of fiction. Among his writings are two feature-length screenplays, *Ai! Pedrito!* and *A Very Strange Trip*. Both screenplays are later adapted and released as full-length novels and become *New York Times* bestsellers. He also produces the largest single-volume science fiction novel ever written, *Battlefield Earth: A Saga of the Year 3000*, and his masterpiece of comic satire, *Mission Earth*—an unprecedented 1.2-million-word science fiction novel in ten volumes, for which he coins the term *dekalogy*.

ENVOI 1982–1986

1982   From his California ranch, Hubbard researches and releases his latest and final discoveries in Scientology. His own literary agency, Author Services, is established and he sees *Battlefield Earth* become an international bestseller after its 1982 release. He composes music and lyrics for *Battlefield Earth*—the first time a recorded "soundtrack" is created to directly accompany a best-selling novel. Shortly thereafter he composes twenty songs for the *Mission Earth* series.

1983   Hubbard launches an international science fiction and fantasy short story and novelette competition for new and aspiring writers, which he calls the Writers of the Future Contest. The Illustrators' Contest is founded in 1988 to encourage the speculative fiction artist in much the same way the Writers' Contest has been doing for authors.

1985   The first volume of L. Ron Hubbard's *Mission Earth* is published in October and becomes an instant bestseller. As each volume of the dekalogy is released through forthcoming years, each becomes a bestseller. The successive appearance of these volumes on the *New York Times* bestseller list constitutes a first in publishing history. Also an international bestseller is the May 1987 reprint of L. Ron Hubbard's first novel, *Buckskin Brigades*. All told, there are twenty-one consecutive bestsellers in the 1980s—more than for any other author.

L. Ron Hubbard passes away on January 24, 1986, but the impact of his literary legacy continues to grow. In response to demands for his work, a twenty-year schedule to republish his earlier fiction and to publish previously unpublished stories is initiated by Author Services. The first two works released, *Final Blackout* and *Fear*, promptly leap onto bestseller lists, repeating their popularity of fifty years earlier and underscoring his enduring stature as a master storyteller.

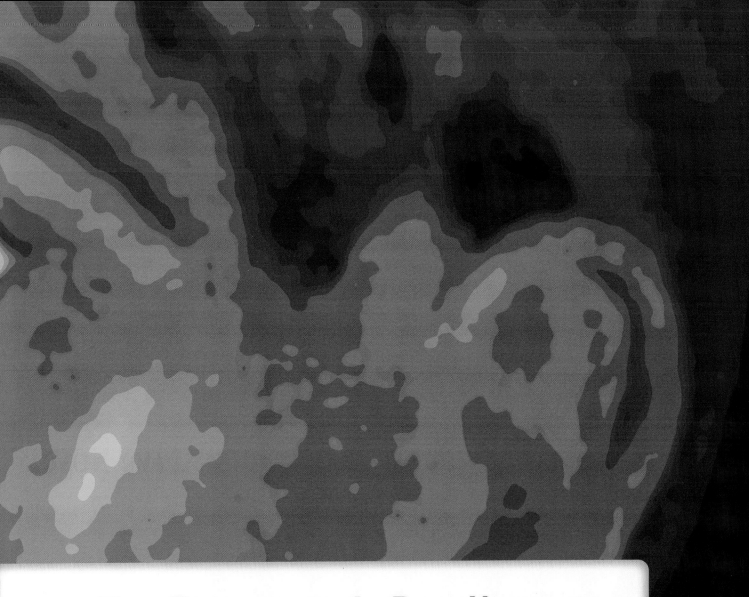

The Fiction of L. Ron Hubbard

The full range of L. Ron Hubbard's huge output of fiction is legendary in its scope, versatility and rich creative energies. From the very beginning of his career as a master storyteller and one of the most widely read—and enduringly popular—writers of our time, his novels and stories captured an indelibly vivid sense of things as they are, or as they were at some watershed moment in history, or as they might be on a future world or at some crucial juncture in time and space.

"Trying harder to make every word live and breathe," as he himself once defined the imaginative intensity of his work, Hubbard poured out a broad stream of fiction—tales of action and adventure, mystery and suspense, the romantic old West and high comedy, science fiction and fantasy, and more. They are, here, listed sequentially, as they appeared over more than five decades of one of the defining careers in American popular fiction.

1932	February	*Tah*
	April	*Grounded*
	May	*The God Smiles*
	November	*Submarine*
1934	February	*The Green God*
	April	*Calling Squad Cars!*
	May	*Pearl Pirate*
	June	*Sea Fangs*
	July	*Dead Men Kill*
	September	*Twenty Fathoms Down*
		Mouthpiece
	October	*Yellow Loot*
	November	*Hurtling Wings*
		The Carnival of Death
1935	January	*The Phantom Patrol*
		The Trail of the Red Diamonds
	February	*The Red Dragon*
		Flame City
	March	*Destiny's Drum*
	April	*Brass Keys to Murder*
	May	*False Cargo*
		The Squad That Never Came Back
		The Drowned City
	May–June	*The Cossack*
	June	*Man-Killers of the Air*
	July	*Hostage to Death*
		Hell's Legionnaire
	August	*The Contraband Crate*
		Under the Black Ensign
		Yukon Madness
	September	*Buckley Plays a Hunch*
		Medals for Mahoney
		The Sky Devil
	October	*He Walked to War*
		Murder Afloat
		Forbidden Gold
		Wind-Gone-Mad

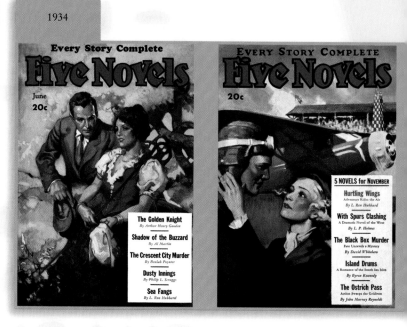

1935

1936

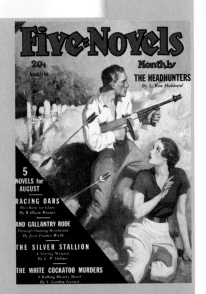

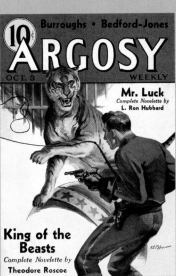

Five Mex for a Million	November
The Adventure of "X"	
The Black Sultan	
The Barbarians	December
Machine Gun 21,000	
Trick Soldier	January **1936**
The Sky-Crasher	
Starch and Stripes	
Red Sand	February
Price of a Hat	March
The Blow Torch Murder	
Hurricane	
Spy Killer	April
The Death Flyer	
They Killed Him Dead	May
Loot of the Shanung	
Escape for Three	June
The Mad Dog Murder	
The Grease Spot	July
Sleepy McGee	
Don't Rush Me	
The Headhunters	August
Sky Birds Dare!	September
The Baron of Coyote River	
The Slickers	
Mr. Tidwell, Gunner	
Golden Hell	
Flaming Arrows	October
Tomb of the Ten Thousand Dead	
Mr. Luck	
Test Pilot	
Deep-Sea Diver	
The Big Cats	
Black Towers to Danger	
The No-Gun Gunhawk	November
River Driver	
The Ethnologist	
Fifty-Fifty O'Brien	December
Mine Inspector	
The Shooter	
While Bugles Blow!	

1937	January	*Steeplejack*
		Flying Trapeze
	February	*Mountaineer*
		The Bold Dare All
	March	*The Battling Pilot*
		Cattle King for a Day
		A Lesson in Lightning
	June	*The Crate Killer*
		All Frontiers Are Jealous
	July	*The Dive Bomber*
		Buckskin Brigades
	August	*Nine Lives*
	September	*Reign of the Gila Monster*
	October	*Red Death Over China*
	November	*The Devil—With Wings*
		Gunman's Tally
		Cargo of Coffins
	December	*Tinhorn's Daughter*
		Orders Is Orders
1938	March	*Six-Gun Caballero*
		Under the Die-Hard Brand
	June	*The Toughest Ranger*
		Arctic Wings
		Killer Ape
	June–July	*Hot Lead Payoff*
	July	*King of the Gunmen*
		The Dangerous Dimension
		Ride 'Em, Cowboy!
	August	*The Ghost Town Gun-Ghost*
		When Gilhooly Was in Flower
	September	*Boss of the Lazy B*
	September–November	*The Tramp*
	October	*Come and Get It*
		Branded Outlaw
		The Lieutenant Takes the Sky
		Death Waits at Sundown
	November	*Silent Pards*
	December	*Ruin at Rio Piedras*
		Empty Saddles

1937

1938

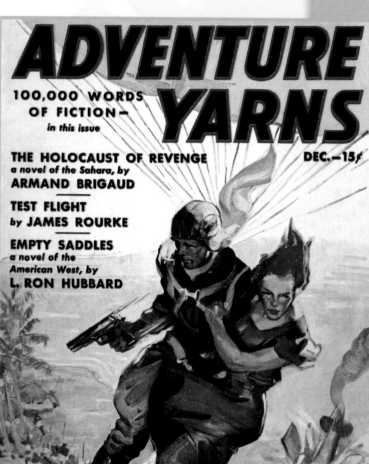

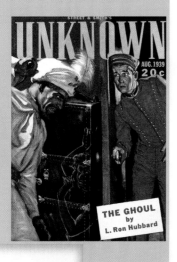

1939

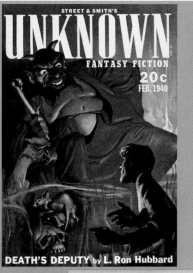

1940

1941

Trouble on His Wings	January	**1939**
Wings Over Ethiopia	February	
The Ultimate Adventure	April	
The Falcon Killer		
Hurricane's Roar		
Danger in the Dark	May	
Slaves of Sleep	July	
The Ghoul	August	
The Ranch That No One Would Buy	October	
The Professor Was a Thief	February	**1940**
The Small Boss of Nunaloha		
If I Were You		
Death's Deputy		
The Indigestible Triton	April	
Final Blackout	April–June	
On Blazing Wings	May	
Shadows From Boot Hill	June	
Inky Odds		
The Iron Duke	July	
Fear		
The Idealist		
Sabotage in the Sky	August	
The Kilkenny Cats	September	
The Devil's Rescue	October	
One Was Stubborn	November	
Typewriter in the Sky	November–December	
The Traitor	January	**1941**
The Crossroads	February	
The Mutineers	April	
The Case of the Friendly Corpse	August	
Borrowed Glory	October	
The Last Drop	November	
The Invaders (a.k.a. *Behind the Black Nebula*)	January	**1942**
He Didn't Like Cats	February	
The Rebels		
Strain	April	
The Room		
The Slaver	June	
Space Can	July	
The Beast	October	

1943 April *The Great Secret*

1947 July *The Chee-Chalker*
August–October *The End Is Not Yet*
September *Killer's Law*
October *Ole Doc Methuselah*
November *The Expensive Slaves*

1948 March *Her Majesty's Aberration*
May *The Obsolete Weapon*
June *The Magic Quirt*
July *When Shadows Fall*
September *The Great Air Monopoly*
December *240,000 Miles Straight Up*
Stacked Bullets

1949 January *Forbidden Voyage*
February *Gunman!*
March *The Magnificent Failure*
April *The Gunner From Gehenna*
Plague!
Gun Boss of Tumbleweed
May *The Conroy Diary*
The Incredible Destination
Battle of Wizards
June *A Sound Investment*
July *The Unwilling Hero*
August *Johnny, the Town Tamer*
A Matter of Matter
September *Beyond the Black Nebula*
Guns of Mark Jardine
Blood on His Spurs
October *The Automagic Horse*
The Planet Makers
November *The Kingslayer*
The Emperor of the Universe
Man for Breakfast
December *Stranger in Town*
A Can of Vacuum

1950 January *Ole Mother Methuselah*
Hoss Tamer
Beyond All Weapons
The Last Admiral

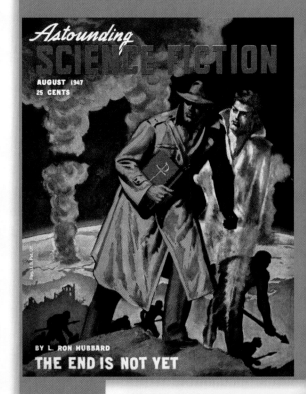

1947

1948

1949

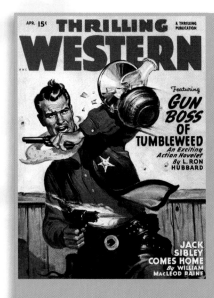

1950

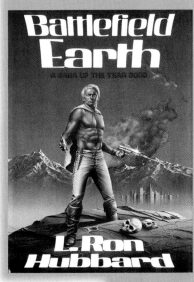

1982

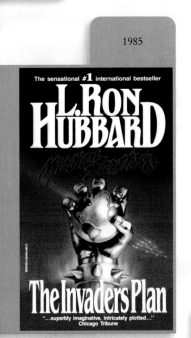

1985

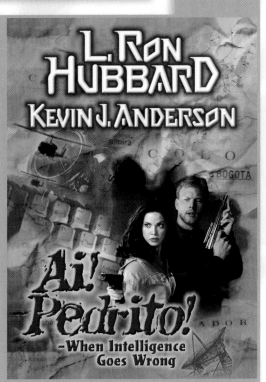

1998

Devil's Manhunt	February	
To the Stars (a.k.a. *Return to Tomorrow*)	February–March	
Greed	April	
The No-Gun Man	May	
Vengeance Is Mine!	June	
Battling Bolto	August	
Final Enemy	September	
The Masters of Sleep	October	
Tough Old Man	November	
The Were-Human	October	**1981**
Battlefield Earth	May	**1982**
He Found God	September	
Mission Earth, Volume 1: The Invaders Plan	October	**1985**
Mission Earth, Volume 2: Black Genesis	March	**1986**
Mission Earth, Volume 3: The Enemy Within	April	
Mission Earth, Volume 4: An Alien Affair	July	
Mission Earth, Volume 5: Fortune of Fear	October	
Mission Earth, Volume 6: Death Quest	January	**1987**
Mission Earth, Volume 7: Voyage of Vengeance	May	
Mission Earth, Volume 8: Disaster	July	
Mission Earth, Volume 9: Villainy Victorious	September	
Mission Earth, Volume 10: The Doomed Planet	November	
Mariner's Mate	June	**1991**
Model Gentleman	January	**1992**
Hired Assassin	June	
Gift From Heaven		
The Secret of Skeleton Creek	June	**1993**
All–South American	July	**1997**
Winged Rescue	September	
Ai! Pedrito!—When Intelligence Goes Wrong	July	**1998**
Witch's Rocking Chair		
A Very Strange Trip	July	**1999**
Stowaway Deluxe	April	**2001**
The Wrecking Crew	December	

POSTSCRIPT

L Ron Hubbard was a man of Renaissance versatility and accomplishment who brought the whole, diverse range of his life into his fiction and into the cultural mainstream of our time. But above all, he was consummately a writer. As he said, writing had never been just his job—it had always been his recreation. And we are all richer for it.

*"My salvation is to let all this roll over me,
to write, write and write some more.
To hammer keys until I am finger worn to the second joint
and then to hammer keys some more.
To pile up copy, stack up stories, roll the wordage
and generally conduct my life
along the one line of success I have ever had.
I write."*

—from L. Ron Hubbard's Journal, January 6, 1944

INDEX

A   *Adventure* —— v, 22–25, 51–52
Adventure Novels —— 3
"Adventure of 'X,' The" —— 185
Adventure Yarns —— 46, 186
*Adventures of the Mysterious
    Pilot, The* —— 52, 54, 173
*Ai! Pedrito!—When Intelligence
    Goes Wrong* —— 34, 124, 181, 189
Albright, Richard —— 13
Alger, Horatio —— 3
"All Frontiers Are Jealous" —— 186
"All–South American" —— 189
All Western Magazine —— 44
Amazing Stories —— 5
American Fiction Guild —— 27, 36,
    145, 172
Anderson, Kevin J. —— 93, 116, 147,
    161, 189
"Arctic Wings" —— v, 22, 186
Argosy —— 3, 7, 26–32, 34, 51–52,
    70, 185
Asimov, Isaac —— 7, 56, 83
Astounding Science Fiction — ii–iii, vi,
    30, 33, 54–60, 65–66, 68, 70, 72–73,
    75, 77–81, 94–103, 105, 108–11, 173,
    178, 186–88
Astounding Stories —— 54
Astounding Stories of Super Science – 54
Author & Journalist —— 146,
    153, 173
Automagic Horse, The —— 105,
    110–11, 188

B   *Baltimore Evening Sun* —— 118, 120
"Barbarians, The" —— 4, 185
"Baron of Coyote River, The" —— 185
"Battle of Wizards" —— 188
Battlefield Earth album —— 125
*Battlefield Earth: A Saga of the
    Year 3000* —— iii, vii, 34, 53, 57,
    79, 91, 104, 113–27, 130, 137, 139,
    173, 178, 181, 189
"Battling Bolto" —— 55, 189
"Battling Pilot, The" —— 186
Beason, Doug —— 147, 161
"Beast, The" —— 94, 187
Benford, Gregory —— 147, 150, 161
*Best of Writers of the
    Future, The* —— 146
"Beyond All Weapons" —— 109, 188
"Beyond the Black Nebula" —— 105,
    107, 188
"Big Cats, The" —— 29, 185
"Black Sultan, The" —— 5, 185
"Black Towers to Danger" —— 18, 185
Blackfeet Indians —— 42–43, 45,
    164–65, 173
Blish, James —— 84
"Blood on His Spurs" —— 178, 188
Bloomfield, Howard V. L. —— 23
"Blow Torch Murder, The" —— 185
Blue Light —— 178
Bodin, Ed —— 88
Bok, Hannes —— 63
"Bold Dare All, The" —— 186
Bonestell, Chesley —— 97, 100–1
Bookwatch —— 139
"Borrowed Glory" —— 187
"Boss of the Lazy B" —— 186
Bova, Ben —— 147, 161

Bradbury, Ray —— 7, 63, 82–84, 159
Bradley, Marion Zimmer —— 105
Brand, Max —— v, 7
"Branded Outlaw" —— 20, 46, 186
"Brass Keys to Murder" — 39–40, 184
"Brass Tacks" —— 73
Brigham, Bill —— 6, 8, 12,
    16, 18, 21, 22, 40
Brigham Young University —— 151
Brim, Jae —— 157
Brooks, Terry —— 147, 161
Brown, Howard V. —— 59–60
"Buckley Plays a Hunch" —— 184
Buckskin Brigades —— v, 30, 43,
    45–46, 51, 173, 181, 186
Budrys, Algis —— 82, 147, 151, 153,
    157, 160–61
Buffalo Bill —— 3
Buffalo Bill —— 5
"Buried Alive" —— 53
Burroughs, Edgar Rice – 7, 27, 36, 172
Burton, Sir Richard —— 59
Byrd, Admiral Richard E. —— 176
Byrne, Jack —— 27

C   "Calling Squad Cars!" —— 38, 184
Campbell, Jr., John W. —— 33, 53,
    55–57, 59–60, 63, 65–66, 70, 77–79,
    83, 96, 102–3, 108–9, 110, 155, 173
Campbell, Ramsey —— 147, 159, 161
"Campfire, The" —— 23–25
"Can of Vacuum, A" —— 188
Captain Blood —— 93
Card, Orson Scott— 131, 139, 147, 161
"Cargo of Coffins" —— 22, 186
"Carnival of Death, The" —— 38, 184
Carter, Nick —— 3, 5
Cartier, Edd —— 62, 64, 66, 71, 76,
    83, 92–94, 96–97, 100–3, 110, 154, 161
*Case of the Friendly
    Corpse, The* — 72, 73, 94, 102, 187
"Cattle King for a Day" —— 44, 186
Chandler, Raymond — 7, 27, 36, 172
"Chat With the Range Boss, A" — 49
"Chee-Chalker, The" —— 22, 95,
    178, 188
Chrissie Dreams of Rescue —— 126
Christie, Agatha —— 7
Clarkson, Andy B. —— 159
Clement, Hal —— 147, 161
Colt, Winchester Remington —— 46,
    88–89
Columbia Pictures —— 52, 54, 173
"Come and Get It" —— 186
Complete Northwest —— 43
Conan —— 27
"Conquest of Space" series —— 79,
    95–96, 104–8
"Conroy Diary, The" —— 188
"Contraband Crate, The" —— 184
Corea, Chick —— 125
Corea, Gayle Moran —— 125
"Cossack, The" —— 184
Countess Krak, The —— 138
Countess, The —— 132
"Crate Killer, The" —— 186
"Crossroads, The" —— 57, 94, 187

D   Daly, Lt. Jonathan —— 89
"Danger in the Dark" —— 60, 187
"Dangerous Dimension, The" – ii, vi,
    46, 56–58, 69, 82, 121, 173, 186
"Dead Men Kill" —— 36, 39, 184
"Death Flyer, The" – ii, v–vi, 39, 56,
    82, 185

Death of a Tolnep —— 125
"Death Waits at Sundown" —— 186
Death's Deputy —— vii, 68, 70–72,
    102, 173, 187
"Deep-Sea Diver" —— 28, 29, 185
Dell Publishing —— 19
"Destiny's Drum" —— 184
Detective Fiction Weekly —— 38–40
Detective Story —— 5
Detective Yarns —— 40
"Devil—With Wings, The" — 20, 186
"Devil's Manhunt" —— 49, 189
"Devil's Rescue, The" —— 187
Di Fate, Vincent —— 154, 161
"Dianetics: The Evolution of
    a Science" —— 178
*Dianetics: The Modern Science of
    Mental Health* —— 110, 178
Dillon, Diane —— 154, 161
Dillon, Leo —— 154, 161
Dime Adventure Magazine — 4, 186
Dimension X —— 69
"Dive Bomber, The" —— 186
"Don't Rush Me" —— 29, 185
"Drowned City, The" —— 184
*Duelist and the Countess
    Krak, The* —— 139

E   Eggleton, Bob —— 152, 158, 161
Eisner, Will —— 158, 161
"Emperor of the Universe, The"— 105,
    107, 188
"Empty Saddles" —— 46, 186
End Is Not Yet, The —— vii, 39, 57,
    95–97, 109, 120, 121, 188
"Escape for Three" —— 185
"Ethnologist, The" —— 29, 185
Everett (Washington) Herald — 129
"Expensive Slaves, The" —— 98, 188
Explorers Club —— 69, 93, 146,
    173–74, 176, 178–79
Explorers Journal —— 177–78

F   "Falcon Killer, The" —— 21, 187
"False Cargo" —— 14, 184
Famous Western —— 47, 49
Fantastic Adventures —— 65
Farmer, Philip José —— 140
Fear —— ii, vii, 57, 68–69, 72–73, 78,
    82–87, 90, 102–3, 139, 173, 181, 187
"Fifty-Fifty O'Brien" —— 185
Final Blackout —— iii, viii, 68–69,
    72–78, 90, 120, 139, 173, 181, 187
"Final Enemy" —— 189
"Five Mex for a Million"— 17, 22, 185
Five Novels Monthly —— v, 4, 6, 8,
    13–14, 20, 22, 39–40, 46, 95, 184–85
"Flame City" —— 184
"Flaming Arrows" —— 185
"Flying Trapeze" —— 29, 186
"Forbidden Gold" —— 15–16, 184
"Forbidden Voyage" —— 105–7, 188
Forester, C. S. —— 27
Frazetta, Frank —— 74, 126, 132, 146,
    148–51, 153, 156–58, 161
Freas, Frank Kelly —— iii, 2, 62, 152,
    155, 157–59, 161
Freas, Laura Brodian —— 158, 161
Futures to Infinity —— 19

G   Gaiman, Neil —— 116
Gardner, Erle Stanley —— 7
George Washington University — 109,
    145, 157, 168–69
Gernsback, Hugo —— 5

"Ghost Town Gun-Ghost, The"— 186
Ghoul, The ——— 63, 66–67, 72 ,187
"Gift From Heaven" ——— 189
Gladney, Graves ——— 61, 67
Glashow, Dr. Sheldon ——— 151
Glencannon's Run ——— 127
"Globe-Trotter, The" ——— 15
"God Smiles, The" ——— 169, 184
Gold Mining Disaster ——— 116
"Golden Hell" ——— 185
"Golden Pen Award" – 146, 173, 175
Gordon, Capt. Charles ——— 5, 89
Grace, Gerry ——— 117, 130–38
Grand Council ——— 136
"Grease Spot, The" ——— 185
*Great Adventures of Wild Bill
    Hickok, The* ——— 52, 54–55, 173
"Great Air Monopoly, The" ——— 98,
    100, 188
"Great Secret, The" ——— 95, 188
"Greed" ——— 189
"Green God, The" ——— 1, 4, 172, 184
Grey, Zane ——— 7
"Grounded" ——— 169, 184
"Gun Boss of Tumbleweed"— 48, 188
"Gunman!" ——— 47, 188
"Gunman's Tally" ——— 186
Gunn, James ——— 93, 137, 140
"Gunner From Gehenna, The" — 188
"Guns of Mark Jardine" – 46, 48, 188

H Hammett, Dashiell — v, 7, 27, 36, 172
Hartwell, David ——— 83
Harvard ——— 145
"He Didn't Like Cats" ——— 187
"He Found God" ——— 189
"He Walked to War" ——— 23, 184
"Headhunters, The" ——— 6, 185
Heinlein, Robert ——— vi, 5, 7, 33, 57,
    65–66, 75, 104, 110, 114
Helena Independent ——— 166
"Hell Job" series ——— v, 22, 26–32,
    34, 70, 105
"Hell's Legionnaire" ——— 184
Hemingway, Ernest ——— 7
"Her Majesty's Aberration" — 98, 188
Herbert, Brian ——— 147, 161
Herbert, Frank ——— 147, 161
Hillary, Sir Edmund ——— 176
"Hired Assassin" ——— 189
Hoffman, Nina Kiriki ——— 147, 161
Holman, Judith ——— 158, 161
Hopkins, Nicky ——— 125
"Hoss Tamer" ——— 46, 178, 188
"Hostage to Death" ——— 14, 184
"Hot Lead Payoff" ——— 44–46, 186
"Howard, Robert E." ——— 7, 27
Hubbard, Capt. L. Ron ——— 89
Hubbel, Bernard ——— 89
"Hurricane" ——— 6, 185
"Hurricane's Roar" ——— 3, 187
"Hurtling Wings" ——— 11, 13–14,
    19, 184

I "Idealist, The" ——— 78–79, 187
"If I Were You" ——— 187
Illustrators of the Future
    Contest ——— 157, 161, 181
In Search of Wonder ——— 94
"Incredible Destination, The" — 106,
    188
Indigestible Triton, The ——— vii, 68,
    73, 75–76, 96, 102, 187
"Inky Odds" ——— 187
Invaders Plan, The ——— 130

"Invaders, The" ——— 94, 187
"Iron Duke, The" ——— 22, 187
Irving, Washington ——— 59–60
Isip, R. ——— 79

J Janitschek, Hans W. ——— 153
Jettero and Hightee Heller ——— 135
Jettero Heller ——— 142
"Johnny, the Town Tamer" ——— 188
Jones, Robert Gibson ——— 65
Jonnie Goodboy Tyler ——— 117
Joy City ——— 142

K Keith, Michael ——— 39–40, 89
Kijima, Shun ——— 119, 127, 158, 161
"Kilkenny Cats, The" ——— 68, 78–79,
    80–81, 94, 105, 175, 187
"Killer Ape" ——— 40, 186
"Killer's Law" ——— 39, 178, 188
"King of the Gunmen" ——— 186
King, Stephen ——— 82–84
Kingslayer, The — 108, 111, 178, 189
Kirby, Jack ——— 158, 161
Knight, Damon ——— 66, 94
Kondo, Dr. Yoji ——— 115
Kotani, Eric ——— 147, 161
Kyle, Richard ——— 30

L L. Ron Hubbard Gallery ——— 160
*L. Ron Hubbard Presents Writers
    of the Future* ——— iii, 145–61
Lafayette, Rene ——— 56, 69, 76,
    88–89, 96–97, 99, 105–8, 164
L'Amour, Louis ——— 7
"Last Admiral, The" — 105, 108, 188
"Last Drop, The" ——— 187
Lawrence, T. E. ——— 168
Learning Machine, The ——— 126
Legend, The ——— 127
Legionnaire 148 ——— 89
Legionnaire 14830 ——— 89
Lehr, Paul ——— 154, 158, 161
"Lesson in Lightning, A"— 29, 32, 186
Lewis, Sinclair ——— 7
"Lieutenant Takes the Air, The."
    See "Lieutenant Takes the Sky, The"
"Lieutenant Takes the Sky, The" — 20,
    22, 46, 186
Lieutenant, The ——— 74
Lindahn, Ron ——— 158, 161
Lindahn, Val Lakey——— 158, 161
London, Jack ——— 7, 45
Long, Karawynn ——— 160
"Loot of the Shanung" ——— 18, 185

M "Machine Gun 21,000" ——— 185
"Mad Dog Murder, The" ——— 39, 185
"Magic Quirt, The" ——— 47, 188
"Magnificent Failure, The" ——— 188
"Man for Breakfast" ——— 188
Man, the Endangered Species ——— 126
"Man-Killers of the Air" — 15, 22, 184
Margulies, Leo ——— 88–89
"Mariner's Mate" ——— 189
Martin, Ken ——— 46, 88–89
Masters of Sleep, The ——— vii, 65, 178,
    189
"Matter of Matter, A" ——— 105, 188
McCaffrey, Anne ——— 139–140, 147,
    157, 161
McChesney, Florence ——— 14
"Medals for Mahoney" ——— 184
Melville, Herman ——— 7, 45

Merriwell, Frank ——— 3
Meyer, Gary — 136, 141–42, 150–51
Meyers, Ilene ——— 136
"Mighty Machine, The" ——— 55
"Mine Inspector" ——— 29, 185
Mission Earth——— iii, vii, 34, 79, 124,
    128–43, 181
Mission Earth music soundtrack — 141
Mission Earth, Volume 1
    The Invaders Plan — 131, 137, 189
Mission Earth, Volume 2
    Black Genesis ——— 131, 189
Mission Earth, Volume 3
    The Enemy Within ——— 131, 189
Mission Earth, Volume 4
    An Alien Affair ——— 132, 189
Mission Earth, Volume 5
    Fortune of Fear ——— 133, 189
Mission Earth, Volume 6
    Death Quest ——— 134, 189
Mission Earth, Volume 7
    Voyage of Vengeance ——— 135, 189
Mission Earth, Volume 8
    Disaster ——— 136, 189
Mission Earth, Volume 9
    Villainy Victorious ——— 137, 189
Mission Earth, Volume 10
    The Doomed Planet — 137–38, 189
Mists of Avalon, The ——— 105
Moby Dick ——— 45
"Model Gentleman" ——— 189
Moebius ——— 158, 161
Moore, C. L. ——— 66, 147, 161
Morgan, Scott
    (*also* Lt. Scott Morgan) ——— 89
Moskowitz, Sam ——— 19, 33
"Mountaineer" ——— 29, 31, 186
"Mouthpiece" ——— 37, 184
"Mr. Luck" ——— 28, 29, 185
"Mr. Tidwell, Gunner" — v, 22, 185
Munsey, Frank ——— 3
"Murder Afloat" ——— 184
Murder at Pirate Castle — 52, 173
Musgrave, Story ——— 153
"Mutineers, The" ——— 80–81, 187
My Best Science Fiction Story ——— 69
Mystery Novels ——— v–vi, 38–39

N NASA Space Center ——— 153
National Geographic ——— 168
Nelson, Ray Faraday ——— 84, 139
New Detective ——— 39
New York Herald Tribune ——— 75
New York Newsday ——— 134
New York Times ——— 43, 52, 115,
    124, 131, 137, 171, 178, 181
Nick Carter ——— 5
"Nine Lives" ——— 29, 34, 186
Niven, Larry ——— 147, 159, 161
"No-Gun Gunhawk, The" — 46, 185
"No-Gun Man, The" ——— 49, 189
Norton, Andre ——— 147, 161
Nugget ——— 166

O "Obsolete Weapon, The"— 70, 178, 188
Old Tom ——— 43
Ole Doc Methuselah — vii, 39, 57, 73,
    79, 95–101, 103, 105, 108, 178, 188
"Ole Mother Methuselah" — 98, 101,
    108, 188
"On Blazing Wings" ——— 8, 187
"One Was Stubborn" ——— 70, 187
"Orders Is Orders" ——— 186

P Page, Norvell ——— 52, 173

Palace City —— 141
Parade of Acts —— 136
"Pearl Pirate" —— 184
Peary, Robert —— 176
Pepperdine University —— 151
Phalen, David —— 155
"Phantasmagoria" —— 82
Phantom Detective —— v, 38
Phantom Duel, The —— 53
"Phantom Patrol, The" —— 12, 19, 184
Pilot —— 8
"Plague!" —— 99, 188
"Planet Makers, The" —— 108, 188
Pohl, Frederik —— 7, 63, 65, 75, 91, 124, 147, 159, 161
Popular Detective —— 38
Portland Journal —— 10
Pournelle, Jerry —— 147, 161
Powers, Tim —— 147, 153, 157, 160–61
Poyarkov, Sergey V. —— 158–59, 161
"Price of a Hat" —— 185
"Professor Was a Thief, The"—— 68, 187
Publishers Weekly —— 118–19
Pursuit —— 119

R "Ranch That No One Would Buy, The" —— 46, 187
Randolph, Barry —— 20, 46, 89
"Rebels, The" —— 79, 81, 187
"Red Death Over China"—— 13, 19, 186
"Red Dragon, The" —— 12, 19, 184
"Red Sand" —— 185
"Reign of the Gila Monster" —— 186
Requiem for Astounding, A —— 72
Return to Tomorrow —— 109, 111, 189
Revolt in the Desert —— 168
Revolt in the Stars —— 180
Reynolds, Capt. Humbert —— 89
"Ride 'Em, Cowboy" —— 186
Rio Kid Western —— 47
"River Driver" —— 29, 31, 185
Robert the Fox —— 116
Rocky Mountain News —— 115
Rogers, Alva —— 72
Rogers, Hubert —— 72, 79–81, 95, 98, 111
Romantic Range —— 46
"Room, The" —— 70, 187
"Ruin at Rio Piedras" —— 186
Rutgers University —— 151

S Sabatini, Rafael —— v, 93
"Sabotage in the Sky" —— 21–22, 187
"Sans Power" —— 171
Schiff, Jack —— 33
Schomburg, Alex —— 158, 161
Science Fiction Quarterly —— 7
Science Fiction Stories —— 95
Scientology —— 178, 181
Scott, H. Winfield —— 62
"Sea Fangs" —— 184
Sea Hawk —— 93
"Secret of Skeleton Creek, The"—— 189
Secret of Treasure Island, The —— 52, 53, 172–73
"Shadows From Boot Hill" —— 46, 49, 187
Sheffield, Charles —— 147, 161
"Shooter, The" —— 29, 185
"Silent Pards" —— 186
Silverberg, Robert —— 52, 82, 98, 147, 161
Sinclair, Upton —— 7
"Six-Gun Caballero" —— v, 46, 186
Sky Birds —— 22

"Sky Birds Dare!" —— 185
"Sky Devil, The" —— 184
"Sky-Crasher, The" —— 185
"Slaver, The" —— 187
Slaves of Sleep —— vii, 57, 60, 62–65, 72–73, 102, 187
"Sleepy McGee" —— 28, 29, 185
"Slickers, The" —— 39–40, 185
"Small Boss of Nunaloha, The" —— 22, 187
Smashing Novels —— 18
Smith, Dean Wesley —— 115
"Sound Investment, A" —— 100, 188
"Space Can" —— 187
Spencer, Joe —— 125, 138
Spider Returns, The —— 52
Spider, The —— 52, 173
Sportsman Pilot —— 169, 171
"Spy Killer" —— 6, 185
"Squad That Never Came Back, The" —— 88, 184
"Stacked Bullets" —— 188
Standard Magazines —— 33
"Starch and Stripes" —— 22, 185
Startling Stories —— 96, 105–8
"Steeplejack" —— 29, 186
Stewart, John —— 116
Stinson, Paul —— 115
"Stowaway Deluxe" —— 189
"Strain" —— 94, 187
"Stranger in Town" —— 188
Street & Smith —— ii, 3, 30, 46, 53–56, 57, 59, 102, 173
Sturgeon, Theodore —— 57, 147, 161
"Submarine" —— 171, 184
Super Science Stories —— 75, 105, 109
"Suspense" —— 146
Sutton, Scott E. —— 111
Swift, Tom —— 3

T "Tah" —— 169, 184
"Tailwind Willies" —— 169
Tales of the Alhambra —— 59
Tales of Wells Fargo —— 46
"Terra Incognita: The Mind" —— 177–78
"Test Pilot" —— 29, 185
"They Killed Him Dead" —— 185
Thompson, Commander Joseph "Snake" —— 164–65
Thrilling Adventures —— 1–2, 4–5, 15, 22, 88, 172
Thrilling Detective —— 36–37, 39
Thrilling Western —— 48–49, 188
Thrilling Wonder Stories —— 105
"Tinhorn's Daughter" —— 186
To the Stars —— vii, 94–95, 108–9, 111, 178, 189
"Tomb of the Ten Thousand Dead" —— 5, 185
Top-Notch —— v, 17, 22, 54, 185
"Tough Old Man" —— 105, 189
"Toughest Ranger, The" —— 46, 186
"Trail of the Red Diamonds, The" - 184
"Traitor, The" —— 80, 187
"Tramp, The" —— vii, 46, 57–60, 69, 82, 121, 186
"Trick Soldier" —— 185
"Trouble on His Wings" —— 17, 20, 187
Tug One —— 134, 143
Twain, Mark —— 7
"Twenty Fathoms Down"—— 4, 19, 184
"240,000 Miles Straight Up" —— 188
Typewriter in the Sky —— vii, 57, 68–69, 85, 90–93, 102, 139, 175, 187

U "Ultimate Adventure, The" —— 59–61, 173, 187

"Under the Black Ensign" - 17, 22, 184
"Under the Die-Hard Brand" —— 44, 186
United Nations —— 151, 153
University Hatchet —— 169, 171
University of Houston —— 151
University of Kansas —— 151
University of Michigan —— 171
"Unkillables, The" —— 75
Unknown —— ii, 57, 59–63, 65–67, 70–71, 73, 76, 78, 83, 85, 90–91, 93–94, 102–3, 173, 187
"Unwilling Hero, The" —— 106, 188

V Valentine, Lewis J. —— 36
Van Dongen, H. R. —— 158, 161
van Vogt, A.E. —— 57, 110, 116, 124, 140
Varley, John —— 147, 161
"Vengeance Is Mine!" —— 189
Very Strange Trip, A —— 34, 124, 181, 189
Vision —— 127
von Rachen, Kurt —— 56, 78–80, 88–89

W *War Birds* —— 19
Warner Bros. —— 52
Warren, Jim —— 119, 126
Warren, Jr., William R. —— 158, 161
Washington Herald —— 169
"Washington's Langley Day" —— 171
Wentworth, K. D. —— 147, 157, 161
"Were-Human, The" —— 189
Western Aces —— 44
Western Action —— 48, 188
Western Story Magazine —— v, 5, 44, 46, 54
Western Yarns —— 46
"When Gilhooly Was in Flower" —— 46, 186
"When Shadows Fall" —— 105, 188
"While Bugles Blow!" —— 19, 22, 185
White Fang —— 45
Wild West Weekly —— 49, 54
Wilkerson, Paul —— 15
Willardson, Dave —— 135, 139
Williams, Tennessee —— 7
Williamson, Jack —— vi, 82, 147, 152, 159, 160
"Wind-Gone-Mad" —— 2, 184
Windsplitter —— 119
"Winged Rescue" —— 189
"Wings Over Ethiopia" —— 187
Winter, Edgar —— 141
Winters, Greg —— 143
"Witch's Rocking Chair" —— 189
Wolfe, Corey —— 116, 126
Wolfe, Gene —— 139, 147, 161
"Wrecking Crew, The" —— 189
Writer's Digest —— 153
Writers' Markets & Methods —— 153
Writers of the Future Contest —— 146–61, 181
Writer's Review —— 153, 173
Wu, Frank —— 159

Y "Yellow Loot" —— 184
"Yukon Madness" —— 4, 184

Z Zelazny, Roger —— 139, 147, 157, 161